"Very well written and expertly researched. You truly do fall in love with Athens, and the illustrations really help to paint the picture. I enjoyed walking down the streets of Athens and getting a feel for the everyday lives of its people over the years. The personalities, values, loves, fears, and motivations, of the citizenry really come through in this telling—more than any other accounts I have read. Each individual story is very readable and the obstacles overcome by these individuals and those around them are amazing. I really felt like I was given great insight to their personalities and the influences each had on the building and rebuilding of Athens and each other. I also enjoyed the complete references should I want to read further. A good read."

—Pam Mooney
Goodreads

"In this engagingly written narrative, Holst describes the character and ambitions of five key individuals, their family histories, and their relationships with each other, as well as with diverse friends and enemies. He shows how these complex but determined personalities combined to shape both Athenian democracy and the development of Greek theatre and philosophy."

—Rick Szostak, Ph.D.
University of Alberta

ALSO BY SANFORD HOLST

PHOENICIAN SECRETS

SWORN IN SECRET

Ancient Athens
Five Intriguing Lives

Socrates, Pericles, Aspasia, Peisistratos & Alcibiades

Sanford Holst

Santorini
Books

On the cover: the painting *Pericles and Aspasia*
in the Studio of Phidias by Louis Hector LeRoux
(1829-1900) as reinterpreted by Eduardo Mon-
tes. The statue shown is the goddess Athena.

Santorini Publishing
14622 Ventura Boulevard, #800
Los Angeles, California 91403

First Edition
Printing: October 2016

        Publisher's Cataloging-In-Publication Data

Holst, Sanford.
    Ancient Athens: five intriguing lives: Socrates, Pericles,
  Aspasia, Peisistratos & Alcibiades / Sanford Holst.

    pages : illustrations ; cm
    Includes bibliographical references and index.
    ISBN: 978-1-945199-01-1
    LCCN: 2016944492

Acknowledgements

Dr. John Camp, Director of the Agora Excavations in Athens, thoughtfully performed a peer review of this book, and provided inspiration that made the work better. I particularly remember the meeting in his office among the archives of the Agora—where we were discussing gray areas in Athenian history—when we took a break to meet with his research team. This was something he did regularly with the students and visiting professors who came to the Agora to work each summer. It gave them a chance to learn not only from his extensive experience but also from each other. You rarely see people that excited and animated about their work and about the wealth of history that surrounded them. His genial, non-judgmental demeanor and detailed insights seem to have inspired many researchers during his decades in the Agora, and I feel fortunate to be one of them.

Acknowledgement and thanks are also due to the following people, who took time amid their professional duties to share with me some of their considerable expertise in areas essential to this research. Their contributions enabled me to correct the earlier drafts of this manuscript and made it a much stronger representation of people's lives and the events that took place. The responsibility for any errors that remain is solely my own.

    Dr. John Papadopoulos, professor in the Department of Classics, UCLA.

    Dr. Maria Liaska, archaeologist with the Ephorate of Antiquities of Athens, Greek Ministry of Culture.

    Dr. James Wright, Director of the American School of Classical Studies at Athens.

    Dr. Anna Maria Theocharaki, Greek archaeologist and noted expert on the ancient city walls of Athens.

    Dr. Konstantina Kaza-Papageorgiou, Greek archaeologist and authority on the excavations at Euonymon and other sites near Athens.

And of course, I thank the heavenly Author who actually writes all books and causes us to bring these works into the world when the time is right.

CONTENTS

Timeline

(Years before Christian era)

571	**Solon** makes his reforms
546	**Peisistratos** becomes tyrant
510	**Cleisthenes** reinstalls democracy
490	**Marathon** battle victory
484	**Themistocles** leads Athens
484	**Aeschylus** wins Dionysia
480	**Thermopylae & Salamis** battles
479	**Plataea** victory
477	**Delian League** formed
472	**Cimon** leads
468	**Sophocles** wins Dionysia
461	**Pericles** leads
456	**Phidias** makes Bronze Athena
450	**Aspasia** arrives in Athens
447	**Parthenon** building begins
441	**Euripides** wins Dionysia
440	**Samos** war
432	**Socrates** at Potidaea
431	**Peloponnesian** war begins
429	**Pericles** perishes
415	**Alcibiades** at Sicily
404	**Athens** falls to Sparta
399	**Socrates** drinks hemlock
366	**Plato** teaches Aristotle
343	**Aristotle** teaches Alexander
323	**Alexander the Great** dies

The Ancient Greek World

Western region

in the Fifth Century BC

Eastern region

Were I to sing the Athenians'
praise, my theme should be the
glory won....[1]

Pindar

FIVE FOR ATHENS

The golden age of Athens was created by many gifted people, and yet among them were five individuals who stood out clearly for the uniqueness of their contributions and the richness of their experiences. Each of these five people shaped part of their city's fortunes and the glories that crowned it, even while enduring dramatic changes in their private life. Their struggles to overcome those personal obstacles not only caused them to grow in stature, but also shed light on fascinating aspects of Athenian society. These uncommon people were Socrates, Pericles, Aspasia, Peisistratos and Alcibiades.

Peisistratos was a controversial early leader of Athens who established the system of theatre contests that gave rise to the dramatic works of Aeschylus, Sophocles and Euripides. Yet he was not celebrated, even in his own city. This happened because he was Athens' first known tyrant, having seized power by overthrowing the young democracy. Yet even that breach aided the people of Athens by causing them to then create a new democracy stronger than the one they had before. He suffered several reverses, but persevered. And he had a tremendous influence on Pericles, who later followed him as the undisputed leader of this city.

Pericles was a force of nature who swept all before him. He led Athens through its glory years and served as one of its greatest generals, statesmen and patrons of the arts. He commissioned the building of the Parthenon and other iconic works that gave shape and substance to Athens' role as one of the cultural centers of the world. Yet in his personal life he had to deal with the tangible threat that he might be perceived as a tyrant and be cast out of the city through *ostracism*, a fate that had befallen his father. And then there was Aspasia, the love of his life. His relationship with her was considered scandalous, but it may actually have helped him in the cut-throat politics of those times.

Aspasia was derided as a sex worker by her rivals, but in fact she was highly talented and accomplished. She became one of the few women to rise to the highest levels of the Greek world, and was believed to have influenced Pericles in some of his memorable works. This was all the more remarkable because she was originally from the city of Miletus and had to struggle even to be accepted in Athenian society. In this she was aided by the fact that her extensive education included elements of philosophy, which caused her life to become entwined with that of the incomparable Socrates.

Socrates, of course, was one of the most influential philosophers who ever lived. He began life as a stonemason and had a long road to walk before reaching that lofty pinnacle of society. But he completed the journey, and through his student Plato he even provided a foundation for our system of higher education in the West. Athens gained a reputation as a "college town" for many years thereafter. Socrates also took time to became the mentor of a head-strong young man named Alcibiades.

Alcibiades grew up as the protégé of Pericles, so it was not too surprising that he became a charismatic general who strongly impacted the Peloponnesian War. His affair with the queen of Sparta naturally had repercussions for himself and for Athens. Yet he was so dominant in battles on land and sea that Athens fell to Sparta only when he was sent away. And in that aftermath the golden age of Athens lost much of its luster.

Their stories yield an intriguing look into the desires, struggles and reality of life as it actually happened in ancient Athens and the Greek world. And the first of those remarkable individuals was Peisistratos. Without question he was an essential part of Athens' rise from its dimly-lit ancient days to the blindingly bright Classical age which followed. To see his story and the early story of Athens, we now go back to those promising days.

ANTIQUITY AND TYRANNY

As the mists of antiquity flowed across the mountainous terrain of Greece, their wisps embraced the sloping hillsides rich with olive trees, grape vines and other fruits of the land. This bounty continued down to the pebble-strewn shore and warm waters of the blue Mediterranean Sea. Among the towns that grew upon this land, like brightly colored flowers amid green fields, was one dedicated to Athena—the goddess of wisdom, courage and inspiration.

Yet this was also a time of raids and looting that despoiled villages and farms alike. Fortunately, among all the towns in the surrounding countryside, the city of Athena had one unique advantage that made it exceptional. This was its high plateau known as the Acropolis—towering 494 feet above the level of the sea.

Whenever raiders attacked, the townspeople quickly made their way to this naturally-protected place of safety and waited for the marauders to pass. This high refuge could be approached *en masse* only from the west because the other three sides were so steep that they were easily defended. A succession of early leaders made these natural fortifications even better by cutting stones from the top of the hill and using them to build thick stone walls that girded the Acropolis on all sides. That made the natural rock and protective walls form virtually a sheer drop from top to bottom.[2]

Their work also had the benefit of making the top of the Acropolis nearly level and suitable for raising buildings. So it became not only a safe retreat in times of trouble but also a religious sanctuary in times of peace.

When the Hellenes spread across the land in those years long past, mythology and history still competed for dominance. In Athens these people wove a rich culture and established a tradition of strong kings to lead them—with the first of those bearing the name of Cecrops. His followers associated him with snakes, and in the whispers of myths handed down through the ages they described him as being half-snake himself.[3] This became so firmly embedded in the traditions of the city that Athena was forever portrayed with the snake of Cecrops by her side.

This great king was said to have presided over the fateful contest between Athena and Poseidon to determine which deity would become the patron god of this city. To influence the judging, Poseidon stood on the Acropolis and struck his trident into the ground, bringing forth a gift of water for the city. But this water was salty like the sea. Athena planted a seed nearby that grew into a massive olive tree, which then yielded food, oil and wood for the city. Athena's gift was said to be of such great value that the city was named after her and she became its patron goddess.

Many hundreds of years later, when Pericles commissioned Phidias to build the magnificent Parthenon, that epic story would be carved in white marble above its tall columns.

In these years of early kings, it was certainly true that the Hellenes in Athens came in contact with the Minoans of Crete. Some of the people and events in those days even became burnished and embellished by ancient storytellers until they became part of the city's cherished mythology.

In these accounts, a hero named Theseus arose in Athens. As a young man he was taken with thirteen other hostages to the city of Knossos on Crete where the king of the Minoans lived in a magnificent palace. It was said that the captives were taken there to be eaten by a creature who was half-man and half-bull, known as the Minotaur. In reality, it was customary in those days to take important hostages from a foreign city that had fought against your city—in order to guarantee that the foreigners would not fight your city again. The fear that those hostages would be killed was enough to prevent further conflict. In fact, Athens itself often took hostages from cities that it fought in Classical times. But the threat of being eaten made a much better story and so the myth grew.

At Knossos the Minotaur was said to have lived in a labyrinth of corridors that had so many twists and turns that no prisoner could ever find their way out. In another demonstration that mythology often contains particles of truth as well as elements of vivid imagination, the Minoan palace at Knossos has been excavated and clearly showed itself to be a confusing rabbit-warren of rooms connected by corridors. It would be easy to imagine visitors getting lost there, though it was not likely to have been built with that purpose in mind.

In the ancient telling of this story, Theseus killed the Minotaur and returned to Athens. There, his irresistible leadership united all the various parts of Attica under the control of Athens. And in fact, that unification did happen.

After the Minoan age, when Mycenaeans ruled the mainland and Crete, archaeological records show that Athens was a major trading center in Attica. This took place long before the Greek dark age and subsequent rise of Homer and Classical Greece. In those days Athens had a large district devoted to making distinctive pottery that was much in demand at many Greek cities. That district is still known today as Kerameikos, from which we get the word ceramics.

During those prosperous Mycenaean times the demand for this pottery was so great that a second district for making it existed not far from Athens' ancient port at Phaleron. This ceramics suburb was known as Euonymon and is today called Euonymeia or Ano Kalamaki. It is one of the most remarkable sites in Europe due to its ancient artifacts that go back to the Neolithic, Mycenaean and Classical periods. It even includes a unique Classical amphitheater of rectangular design.

Fig. 1 Theseus slaying the Minotaur

The truly surprising thing about this historic site is how little excavation work has been done so far. The most detailed recent work occurred when the Alimos subway station was built there in 2006, causing the unearthing of a sophisticated ceramics workshop and waterworks. The ancient theater stands about 900 feet southwest of the station, and there is another site to the north. A nearby hill is believed to have served as the protective acropolis for Euonymon.[4] Building the metro station impacted the remains of this mostly-unexplored ancient town, but a saving grace was that it made visiting the sites easy to do from anywhere in Athens.

The heads of the leading Hellenic families who established themselves in Euonymon and all the other towns across Attica traveled often to Athens or took up residence there and became power brokers in the city. In the course of doing this they gave rise to the great families or *Eupatridae*, which meant "offspring of noble fathers." Sometimes the word "aristocrats" has been used to describe them. In any event, the kings of Athens came from among these families.

One of those great families, the Alcmaeonids, was particularly significant. This was due to the fact that they produced a number of important leaders in the city, with the most notable one being Pericles.

Strangely enough, it was these great families who gave Athens its first push toward democracy. They did this by taking several steps in the eighth century BC to limit the power of the king. This eventually forced his authority to be divided among three leaders known as *archons*.

The *archon eponymos* became the city administrator, the *polemarch* (from *pólemos archon*) served as military leader, and the *archon basileus* presided over religious rituals and homicide trials. But this was a very limited step because the *archons* were still selected from among the great families.

A powerful council called the Areopagus also came into being at this time. Its members were the past *archons* after they had served in office. To them was given the role of electing the new *archons*—which kept control of the city completely in the hands of the great families.

Fig. 2 Large krater from Euonymon, circa 725 BC

Fig. 3 Solon

With crops and goods from all over Attica coming to Athens' marketplace—the Agora—the city thrived and its population grew. But at first this wealth did not accrue to all. The great families became even more wealthy and owned vast amounts of the countryside. At the same time, many among the rest of the people were reduced to grinding poverty as renters of land—and they became mired in debt from which they could not escape.

This caused incendiary amounts of friction in the community. Worried that a revolution was about to erupt, the power brokers of the city turned to a man named Solon.

Young Solon was born around 638 BC[5] into a *Eupatridae* family that was rich in name but relatively poor in purse. So he made his way in life as a soldier. Solon rose in the ranks until he became commander of the Athenian forces in their war with the city of Megara, fighting for ownership of the island of Salamis. After his victory in 595 BC and the acquisition of Salamis, he returned to Athens and was rewarded the next year with the highest office in the city, that of *archon eponymos*. He was found to be uniquely qualified by the circumstances of his birth to understand the concerns of the rich and the poor in the city, and he eloquently expressed them. So all the various factions eventually agreed to follow his lead in reforming the laws of the city to meet those concerns.[6]

After listening to all the citizens, Solon proposed throwing out the harsh laws introduced by Draco a generation earlier[7]—from which we got the expression of something harsh being "draconian"—and replaced them with laws that were more reasonable. For people crushed with debt, his laws prohibited forcing them into slavery—and in fact it forgave debts of all kinds. This made him almost a patron saint among the poor, but made him less popular among his fellow members in the great families who were the owners of those debts.

Yet many wealthy citizens also benefited, because he proposed opening all the high offices of the city to any citizen who could meet certain standards of wealth. As a result those offices were no longer held solely by the great families, but could go to merchants or other families that had become rich over the years as the city grew.

Ancient sources indicate that Solon also instituted another major change by creating a city council of 400 citizens called the *boule*. Its members were chosen by lot, and were limited to a lower set of responsibilities than those enjoyed by the aristocratic Areopagus. But at least this council began to involve regular citizens more directly in the governing of their city.[8]

While many people in Athens were happy with these changes, some were decidedly unhappy. Feeling caught in the middle of strong passions, Solon announced that he would travel outside the city for ten years, leaving the citizens to work together and iron out their problems. His voluntary departure from the city may well have been the inspiration for a later practice called *ostracism* in which controversial city leaders were voted out of the city for a ten-year cooling off period. Be that as it may, even Solon's travels were somewhat extraordinary.

He was said to have gone to Egypt and visited the pharaoh, Amasis II,[9] then discussed philosophy with the priests of Heliopolis and Sais.[10] After that he helped one of the kings of Cyprus establish his capital city. Then finally Solon spent time with rich King Croesus at Sardis in Lydia, a country whose borders touched the eastern shore of the Aegean Sea.

With those ten years completed, Solon returned home to Athens and found its citizenry divided into three competing political parties. The *Pedieis* owned large properties on the plains of Attica and included the wealthier citizens. The *Hyperakrioi* were the "men of the hills" who counted among their number the poorest people in Attica. And the last group was the *Paralioi* who lived along the coast and made moderate livings with fishing and trade.

In 560 BC Solon's relative Peisistratos[11] usurped power in Athens with the help of the impoverished "men of the hills" and declared himself tyrant. Outraged at the destruction of all he had wrought, the now-elderly Solon swung into action. He went to the Agora and urged all who would listen to oppose this trampling of the laws of the city by his distant cousin.[12] Peisistratos was eventually ousted and the rule of law returned to Athens.

Solon died within two years of his protests. That meant he did not live long enough to see Peisistratos return and successfully install himself as tyrant.

As important as those events were, politics did not encompass all of Greek life at that time. People worked, raised families, and made their way in the world with appropriate offerings to their gods. A few public festivals also helped to ease their burdens. And among the most significant of these relief-valves was the popular Dionysia festival.

This celebration was dedicated to Dionysos[13] as the god of grape harvests, wine, fertility, ritual ecstasy and theatre, so it was only natural that the first erotic festivals in his name originated in the rural countryside. They were timed to coincide with the clearing of the wine. This final fermentation stage usually occurred just after the winter solstice in December, when new wine became available. Sometimes described as drunken orgies, there were actually two different celebrations in honor of Dionysos—one public and one private.

The public ceremony of this Rural Dionysia always began with a procession (*pompe*) in which fertility was celebrated by people carrying aloft wooden or bronze phallus images on long poles (*phallophoroi*). They were accompanied by young girls carrying baskets (*kanephoroi*), people carrying long loaves of bread (*obeliaphoroi*), other people bearing jars of water (*hydriaphoroi*), still others brought jars of wine (*askophoroi*), or carried other offerings (*skaphephoroi*).[14]

After this procession, the Rural Dionysia had competitions involving songs and dancing. Choruses performed *dithyrambs*, which combined music, poetry and dance—sometimes in a wild and ecstatic manner—in honor of Dionysos.

Privately, there were ceremonies involving erotic initiation rituals by which individuals became inducted into the Dionysian Mysteries. Since it was a society in which its members were sworn to secrecy, most of what we know about their practices and traditions has come from depictions in art and written references from that time. The cult images showed Dionysos as a naked or half-naked man holding a *thyrsos* wand made from the stalk of the

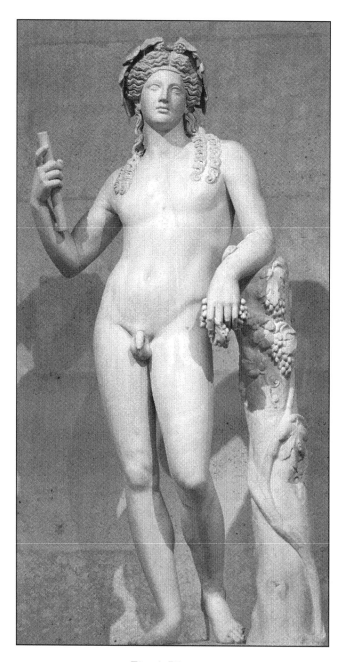

Fig. 4 Dionysos

fennel plant topped by a pine cone. He was usually portrayed making an arrival or return from a foreign place, leading a procession of wild female followers (*maenads*) and bearded satyrs with erect penises.[15] Some of his followers carried *thyrsos* wands while others danced or played music. Dionysos was sometimes shown in a chariot drawn by exotic animals such as tigers or lions.

The original rituals apparently involved drinking wine—possibly enhanced by additives to raise the alcohol and hallucinogenic content—allowing the spirit of Dionysos to possess the participant. The object was to remove all constraints and inhibitions, allowing the participants to be in a more natural state, free of social restrictions. Masks were used by participants in these rituals as they played their roles.[16] In fact a short column with a mask attached to it was sometimes used to represent Dionysos.

These rituals were especially appealing to those people who were subject to serious social limitations in ancient Greece, including women, slaves and foreigners. In their ecstatic, dancing state, all were equal in their enjoyment of life.

At the dawn of Classical Athens there were apparently different rituals for a male initiate and a female initiate. The man was believed to have played the role of Dionysos in his life, death and rebirth. He descended into Hades to retrieve someone or something, then returned through some ordeal to the world above with a greater appreciation of life. Then he shared wine with the gods—possibly in excess and with the hallucinogens added. After that he was shown the secret contents of the *liknon* basket, was presented with his *thyrsos* wand, and was called Bacchus—the alternate name for Dionysos.

Women initiates were said to play the role of Ariadne, the bride of Dionysos. She joined him in the underworld before experiencing an ordeal and returning to the upper world with new insights. At that point she shared wine with the gods—possibly in excess until the proper state was reached—then was shown the contents of her *liknon* basket, which originally contained a goat's penis before being replaced in later times with a wooden phallus. Since the women's initiations were believed to have taken place at the same time as the public celebrations, she was then released to join the ecstatic dancing.

The people of rural Attica, who lived closer to the earth than their city brethren, had embraced these rituals for hundreds of years while the city dwellers held off. But Athenians were well aware that this festival was happening, and were said to have journeyed out to the rural Dionysia held in each small town, where they enjoyed the drinking, dancing and celebrations.

Legend has it that when the town of Eleutherai on the western border of Attica decided to swear loyalty to Athens, they sent their ancient wooden image of Dionysos to Athens as a gift, but it was not accepted. As a result, Dionysos was reported to have punished the men of Athens by striking them with a plague affecting their genitalia. Miraculously, when they changed course and accepted the gift, that plague went away. So each year after that the people of Athens had their own informal procession and celebration, which came to be called the City Dionysia.

That was the relatively crude state of this festival up to the time of Peisistratos, but it would soon change dramatically.

PEISISTRATOS

The privileged family into which Peisistratos was born held large amounts of land in the Philaidai region to the east of Athens near the Mediterranean coast. It was there that his father Hippocrates[17] drummed into him the notion that he was special, citing claims that his family was descended from the legendary Nestor, king of Pylos.[18] Hippocrates even gave this young lad the same name as one of Nestor's children, Peisistratos.

To establish himself, this newer Peisistratos went into military service and reportedly served under his distant relative Solon in that famous campaign which wrested the island of Salamis from the people of Megara. In retribution, Megara launched a sea-trade embargo against Athens, seriously reducing the amount of food flowing into the city. This increased the misery of poorer Athenians, whose talk of rebellion caused the wealthy members of the Areopagus to empower Solon, leading to his reforms. Some years later, while the food embargo dragged on, Peisistratos took advantage of this situation and successfully attacked Nisaia, the main port of Megara. By so doing he forced that city-state to lift its embargo against Athens around 565 BC.

This made Peisistratos incredibly popular among people at all levels of Athenian society, but especially among the long-suffering

*Fig. 5 King Nestor and his sons, believed to be ancestors
of Peisistratos, shown on an Attica krater.*

poor. It also seemed to reinforce the belief taught to him since childhood, that it was his family's destiny to rule. Seeing this opportunity, he began his campaign to become tyrant over the affairs of Athens.

For five years Peisistratos struggled to gain the upper hand in Athenian politics but was thwarted by his opponents. So finally he hit upon an ingenious plan, as told to us by Herodotus.

> When there was a factional dispute between the people of the coast, whose leader was Megacles the son of Alcmaeon, and the people of the plain, led by Lycurgus the son of Aristolaïdes, Peisistratos—with his mind set on tyranny—formed a third party. He gathered his supporters together and made himself appear to be the leader of the hill people.
>
> Then he put the following plan into effect. He wounded himself and his mules and drove his cart into the city square, making it seem as though he was trying to escape from some enemies who had set upon him with murderous intent (or so he said) as he drove out of town. He asked the Athenian people to provide him with personal guards; he had already won their respect as a military commander during the campaign against Megara, during which not the least of his important achievements was the capture of Nisaia. The Athenian people were completely taken in by his trick and chose from among the citizen body some men to give him—that is, those who became his club-carriers, if not his spear-carriers, because they followed him around carrying wooden clubs.
>
> Peisistratos started an uprising with their help and together they took control of the Acropolis. After that, Peisistratos ruled Athens....

> Herodotus
> *Histories 1:59*

Yet this was a short-lived triumph. Megacles and Lycurgus quickly made up their differences and united their parties, using that combined power to drive Peisistratos out of the city. Even so, this solution was only temporary. Infighting between Megacles and Lycurgus soon set party against party again. In fact it was that internal fighting which gave Peisistratos his next opening.

> Megacles was coming off worst in the dispute, and so he sent a message to Peisistratos, asking him whether he would consider marrying his daughter in order to become tyrant. Peisistratos accepted the offer and agreed to his terms. Now, the trick that he and Megacles played in order to bring about his return was by far the most simple-minded one I have ever come across…. There was a woman called Phya in the deme [city district] of Paeania who was only three fingers short of four cubits [about six feet] tall and was also very good-looking. They dressed this woman up in a full set of armour, put her on a chariot, and, after showing her how to hold herself in order to give the most plausible impression, set out for the city with her. Runners were sent ahead to act as heralds, and they, on arriving in the city, made the announcements they had been told to make. 'Men of Athens,' they said, 'Athena is giving Peisistratos the singular honour of personally escorting him back to your Acropolis. So welcome him.' They took this message from place to place, and word soon reached the country demes that Athena was bringing Peisistratos back. Meanwhile, the city-dwellers were so convinced that the woman was actually the goddess that they were offering prayers to her—to a human being—and were welcoming Peisistratos back.
>
> So this was how Peisistratos became tyrant again.
>
> Herodotus
> *Histories 1:60-61*

However the bargain Peisistratos had made quickly came back to haunt him. Having married into the influential Alcmaeonid family which would one day produce Pericles, all he had to do was consummate the marriage by producing a child to cement the agreement. But because he already had two grown sons to inherit his newly-gained authority, he would be taking a great risk by producing an Alcmaeonid heir who might challenge their birth-right. So he refused to consummate the marriage, and "did not have sex with her in the usual way."[19]

Needless to say, Megacles became outraged at the unacceptable treatment of his daughter and the breaking of their agreement. So he immediately opened talks with Lycurgus on how they could rid the city of their tyrant.

When Peisistratos got wind of this danger he fled from Athens and took up residence in exile again, settling in the city of Eretria just north of Attica.

Having failed twice to establish himself as tyrant, Peisistratos worked hard to guarantee that his third attempt would be suc-cessful. He began by collecting contributions of wealth from all who owed his family money or favors. He then recruited merce-naries from the Argos region and put them together with a volun-tary force of men from the island of Naxos.[20]

Thus prepared, he marched into Attica during 546 BC and took the city of Marathon in a show of force. This excited his former supporters, who came from all over Attica to join his campaign. Having assembled a great army, he then began his march on Ath-ens. Not wanting to fight inside the city, the Athenians pulled together their entire body of soldiers and confronted Peisistratos at the sanctuary of Athena in Pallene. An oracle's prophesy in-spired Peisistratos to attack unexpectedly while the Athenian sol-diers were at their mid-day meal, and he routed them completely. All that remained was a victory march into the city.

This time he assured himself of permanent control in Athens by strong use of his mercenary troops. He seized the children of numerous influential Athenians and sent them to the island of Naxos as hostages.

To the Alcmaeonids, who had thwarted his plans twice before, he gave a taste of their own medicine by exiling them from the city. One of these Alcmaeonids was the teenage son of Megacles named Cleisthenes, who was destined to return from exile in spectacular fashion. Another was his brother Hippocrates, whose grandson Pericles would have an even greater destiny.

With that, Peisistratos became master of the town and the Acropolis. The democracy of Athens had given way to tyranny.

Even so, it was clear that the dissident part of the population might still rise up against him as they had done before. So Peisistratos gradually took steps to bring a more populist approach to his rule.

To help the people of the hills who had supported him, he placed a tax on all the agricultural produce of the countryside, then used those funds to help impoverished people obtain small farms of their own. After that he instituted traveling judges to bring redress of injuries to poor people in the country who could not afford to come to the city seeking justice. And within the city of Athens he began catering to the desires of the general public by offering generous support for festivals, games and services.

He noticed in particular that the Dionysia was highly popular among the people of the outlying hills and valleys. Yet in the city it was just one of many cults and festivals. Being a shrewd man, he looked for some way to take advantage of this situation.

Peisistratos wisely used his authority as tyrant to formalize the City Dionysia and place it under the *archon* of the city.[21] By so doing, he gave the festival full municipal funding and support.

Among the popular practices added to the Dionysia at this time was the arranging of competitions among the choral groups, and encouraging original material for each "play." A competing writer would create three short plays with a common theme and have his choral group present them to the public, one after the other. It soon became customary to follow those serious works with an enjoyable "satyr" play of bawdy satire in which the chorus dressed as satyrs and sometimes used a phallus as a prop. This kept the performances in the joyful spirit of the Dionysian rituals and celebrations.

The first time this competition was held, the prize went to a man named Thespis in 534 BC for his plays in which he starred as

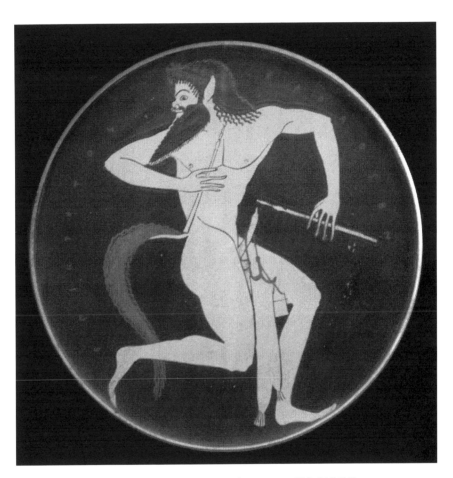

Fig. 6 Satyr on an Attica plate, circa 520-500 BC.

the actor.[22] In honor of his accomplishments, actors are still called thespians to this day. And since the "secret object" in the Dionysian ritual was a goat penis, the prize given to him was a whole goat. That led to this type of play being called a tragedy, from the Greek *tragos oide* or "goat song."

As we will soon see, this city sponsorship of the Dionysia would lead to people devoting substantial parts of their life to writing and performing these plays, giving rise to great playwrights such as Aeschylus, Sophocles, Euripides, Aristophanes and all their memorable works. These in turn gave us the whole world of theatre that has come down to us through the ages.

And it all happened because a tyrant wanted to please and entertain the people of Athens—and allow himself to remain in power.

As it turned out, the transition of Peisistratos from tyrant-at-the-head-of-an-army to benefactor-of-the-people was extremely successful for him. The visible result of this was that most Athenians—even though their rights were strongly curtailed—made no objection to his rule.

And under that rule the foundation of arts, which would contribute to Athens' golden age, continued to grow.

In addition to the Dionysia, Peisistratos made certain that many other festivals filled the city's calendar, and gave those celebrations his generous support.

For the city's Panathenaia festival he made a particularly noteworthy contribution by introducing performances by *rhapsodes*, the singers of epic poetry, who recited the works of Homer. In fact he was said to have sponsored the first permanent writing and archiving of Homer's poems the *Iliad* and the *Odyssey*, which then became the definitive version of those epic works. Prior to that time these epics had been passed along verbally from one *rhapsodos* to another.

A central part of the Panathenaia festival was the grand procession through the heart of the city which ended on the Acropolis at the cult center for *Athena Polias* (Athena in her role as the protector of the city). He upgraded that cult center tremendously by beginning construction of what would come to be known as the Old Temple of Athena located directly in the middle of the Acropolis.

Since Peisistratos had grown up near the town of Brauron four-teen miles east of Athens—where there was a famous Temple of Artemis—he built a sanctuary on the Acropolis dedicated to that goddess. It was more of a stoa than a temple, and stood immediately on the right of the entrance to this sacred plateau. Remnants of the sanctuary to Artemis Brauronia can still be seen today.

Down in the city, Peisistratos further catered to the general public by providing a service greatly needed by them: water. The wealthier citizens were able to build and maintain their own wells. Everyone else had to make trips to the Eridanos River in the northern part of the city, or the Ilissos River in the south. Their benevolent tyrant organized a public works project that built an aqueduct and brought water right into the city. Among the projects attributed to him was a small fountainhouse on the Agora's southeastern corner where anyone could come and draw water.[23]

About 550 feet to the west, archaeologists discovered a large and elaborate building at the southwest corner of the Agora where Peisistratos may well have lived, along with his bodyguards and administrative personnel. But insufficient evidence remains to definitely place him there. The round Tholos building and other structures would later be built directly on top of this old structure, as if to symbolically as well as physically replace the old with the new. But that was still in the future.

A Whip Strikes, Democracy Rises

In 527 BC, Peisistratos passed away and handed the reins of tyranny over to his two sons, Hippias and Hipparchus. These two young men had spent many years growing up with power. They did not have to struggle to win the support of the people as their father had done, but had great power given to them. So they treated people imperiously, as they believed was their right.

They completed the Old Temple of Athena on the Acropolis since it not only reflected glory upon the goddess, but also upon their family. In a deed of their own making, however, they went down to the place southeast of the Acropolis where their father had built a small temple to Olympian Zeus and destroyed that new structure, believing it to be insufficient. In its place they ordered a huge foundation to be laid which could accommodate the largest temple ever built in Greece. The project was so extensive that it could not be completed in their lifetime. Eventually it was abandoned after only a few massive columns had been raised upon the bare platform.

These two men made so many enemies in the city that a plot eventually got under way to kill them. But events went awry and

Fig. 7 Temple of Olympian Zeus

only Hipparchus died in the attack. This convinced Hippias that he was surrounded by real and imagined enemies, and he became a tyrant in the worst sense of the word.

> After this event the tyranny became much harsher. In consequence of his vengeance for his brother—and of the execution and banishment of a large number of persons—Hippias became a distrusted and an embittered man. About three years after the death of Hipparchus, finding his position in the city insecure, he set about fortifying Munychia [Hill at Piraeus], with the intention of establishing himself there.
>
> Aristotle
> *Athenian Constitution 19*

In the midst of this rising tension, the democratic partisans of Athens found a gifted leader in the person of Cleisthenes, the exiled son of Megacles. Since he and Pericles were so important to creating the golden age of Athens, it is worth taking a moment to see the story of the Alcmaeonid family from which they sprang and the heritage that shaped their lives.

According to the lore of the city, the Alcmaeonids were believed to be descended from the early kings of Athens.

When those kings had their power limited by the creation of the high office of *archon*, the last king's son became *archon* for life. That line of hereditary *archons* continued until it reached Alcmaeon, who died in 753 BC. This noble family thereafter took its name from him. The *archons* who followed Alcmaeon were not hereditary, but instead held their office for only ten years. Seventy years later another limitation was made upon those leaders: each *archon* was allowed to hold office for only one year.

In 632 BC a dramatic change happened for the Alcmaeonid family when Megacles—a popular name in their family—was serving his year as *archon*. A man named Cylon made a failed attempt to become tyrant of Athens, and some of his supporters took refuge at an altar. The tyrant's supporters were promised that if they left the sanctuary they would face trial but would not be killed. Yet once they were out in the open they were slain. Megacles was blamed for those deaths and expelled from the city, with a stain being put upon the name of his family for violating that sacred promise.

Even so, his son Alcmaeon—another popular name in this ancient family—earned back the good graces of Athens by commanding its contingent in the First Sacred War to defend the Oracle of Delphi. Leading the allies in that war was a man named Cleisthenes—grandfather to the famous Athenian—who was the wealthy tyrant of Sicyon, a city to the west of Corinth. The two leaders gained much respect for each other in that fighting, so when it became time for Cleisthenes' daughter[24] to marry, her hand was given to Alcmaeon's son Megacles.

This was the same Megacles who gave Peisistratos so many difficulties. Even before that marriage raised his stature higher, Megacles was already leader of the people-of-the-coast, the moderate faction in Athens. So to some extent he became the kingmaker of the city. Each time Megacles gave his support, Peisistratos became tyrant. Each time he withdrew that support, the tyrant was driven out.

That was why, when Peisistratos returned and became permanent tyrant of Athens, he secured his position by driving the whole Alcmaeonid family out of the city. It was not known where young Cleisthenes and his family went to live at that point, but a

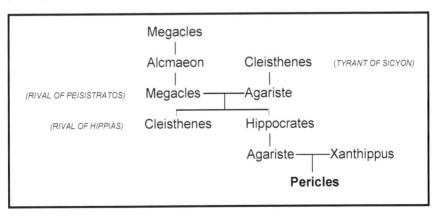

Fig. 8 Pericles' Family — The Alcmaeonids

Fig. 9 The Oracle at Delphi

return to his mother's home in Sicyon has been frequently mentioned.

Cleisthenes grew to maturity during the nineteen years of Peisistratos' reign. Then, when the tyrant's sons took over and conditions began to deteriorate in Athens, he swung into action.

His first steps in this direction were taken at Delphi after a fire destroyed the famous temple of Apollo where the Oracle resided. Cleisthenes' wealthy and influential family offered to perform a complete reconstruction of the temple, and carried it out beautifully. While those much-lauded services were being performed, Cleisthenes used the goodwill thus earned to influence the priests of the Oracle. As a result the Oracle instructed the Spartans repeatedly that they should free Athens from its tyrant.

This tactic was chosen because the Spartans were acknowledged as one of the greatest military forces in Greece at that time. And the leaders of Sparta took pride in using that force in a semi-imperial way to impose their will on different Greek cities if one of the local parties called on them to intervene. Since Cleisthenes and his allies did not have the military strength to drive the tyrant's well-established forces out of the city, this became their best and most promising way forward.

Finally in 510 BC, after constant pressure by the Oracle, the Spartans acted. Their king Cleomenes came north with a large force.

> Cleomenes and the Athenian partisans of freedom made their way to the city, where they pinned the tyrants inside the Pelasgian Wall and began to besiege them there.
>
> Under normal circumstances, there is no way in which the Lacedaemonians [Spartans] would have got the Peisistratidae out of there. The Peisistratidae had plenty of food and water, and the Lacedaemonians had not planned on a siege, so they would have kept up the blockade for a few days and then gone back to Sparta. What happened, however, was a piece of luck which was as bad for one side as it was helpful to the other: the children of the Peisistratidae were captured

as they were being secretly taken out of the country. This threw the Peisistratidae in complete disarray, and in order to recover the children they were forced to surrender on whatever terms the Athenians wanted, which were that they should be out of Attica within five days. And so they left and went to Sigeum on the Scamander River. They had ruled over Athens for a total of thirty-six years.

Herodotus
Histories 5:64-65

So the tyrants were finally gone. That left two rivals for control of Athens: Isagoras who supported the tyrants, and Cleisthenes who advocated a return to democracy. Isagoras persuaded the remaining Spartans that the stain on the Alcmaeonids had never been lifted, so their expulsion from the city should still be enforced. When the Spartans re-entered the city to perform this act, Cleisthenes and his family fled before them.

With the Spartan force supporting him, Isagoras tried to dissolve the city council and have all the power of Athens invested in him and 300 of his friends. The citizens of the city were outraged and drove Isagoras and the Spartans all the way to the Acropolis. Trapped and denied food, Isagoras and the foreign soldiers agreed to leave Athens and were escorted out. Cleisthenes was then recalled to the city and given a hero's welcome.

With the faith and trust of the people invested in him, Cleisthenes set about creating a new government for Athens. What he produced was even more democratic than anything they had experienced before. This step, taken in 508 BC, has generally been regarded as the beginning of full democracy in Athens.

While holding this popular mandate in his hands, Cleisthenes eliminated several of the severe social problems that once divided his city and had opened the door to tyranny. He re-organized the voting system so that each person resided in one of ten voting groups or *phylai*—often referred to as tribes—with each group including some people from the hills, from the plains and from

Fig. 10 Cleisthenes

the coast. He expanded the city council from 400 members to 500, allowing each of the ten districts to send 50 members. In addition, the ten districts each were able to choose a general or *strategos* to lead their soldiers—with the commanding general or *polemarch* for the city being chosen from among them. Other city offices were likewise distributed among citizens from all ten of the districts.

By erasing the old dividing lines of wealth and family groups, he caused people from different backgrounds to work together each day. As a result they started to develop a new, more unified view of themselves as citizens of Athens.

And the large number of poorer citizens in Athens, thus empowered, finally felt like they were part of the electorate, with full rights like any other citizen.

Freed from internal upheavals that had racked them in the past, the people of Athens began to prosper. And their new-found wealth allowed them to fill their leisure time by supporting playwrights, poets, sculptors and musicians. The poet Simonides lived and wrote in Athens during these years. Public festivals soon overflowed with new plays and music. Writers came to read their creations in public. And all of these things helped pave the way for an explosion of the arts that would take place during the city's golden age.

But the true greatness of Athens would not come in Cleisthenes' time—that honor was left to another member of his family. While he was busy making those new laws, his brother Hippocrates had already given birth to a daughter named Agariste, named in honor of the infant's illustrious grandmother.

Agariste was still a young maiden when she married the well-established Athenian general Xanthippus, who went on to distinguish himself in many wars. She proved to be a wonderfully capable wife and mother, for she presented her husband with a daughter and three sons.[25] Then she raised them in a manner that brought great credit to her house, for her youngest son—born in 495 BC—was Pericles.

MARATHON AND PERSIANS

When Pericles was only five years old the epic Battle of Marathon was fought on the eastern shore of Attica. This monumental clash in 490 BC between Greeks and Persians took place within a day's march of Athens. And the aftermath of this battle would affect everything that Pericles accomplished during his extraordinary life. But to fully experience this turning point we need to step back 56 years to the arrival of Persian armies in Anatolia and their first direct contact with the Greeks.

In 546 BC the Persian armies of Cyrus the Great came north and conquered the Anatolia plateau all the way to the east side of the Aegean Sea. They sacked Sardis and the other Lydian cities of King Croesus. Then they swept over many Greek cities arrayed along the coast, including Miletus and Ephesus.

The Persian governor of these newly-captured lands established himself at Sardis and proceeded to appoint a pliable Greek leader to rule as tyrant in each Greek city under his control. The people of those cities adjusted to these unfortunate circumstances, and life went on. But the ongoing friction caused a revolution to flare up in 499 BC.

Those troubles began when Aristagoras, the Greek tyrant of Miletus, decided to attack the island of Naxos using military sup-

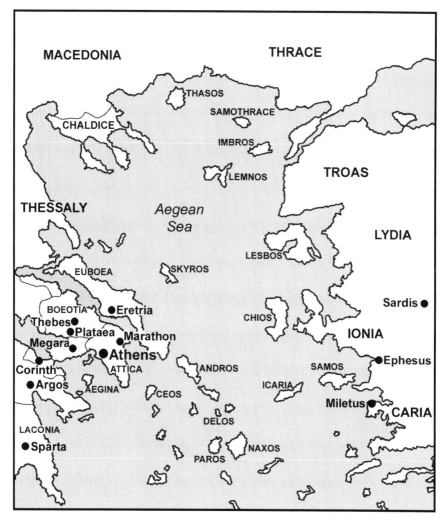

Fig. 11 Greece at the outbreak of the Persian War

port from the Persian governor. Two hundred Persian ships were quickly filled with Aristagoras' men and set sail for Naxos in the middle of the Aegean Sea. But that venture turned into a disaster. And when the survivors of this army returned to Miletus in defeat, Aristagoras was certain he would be replaced as tyrant of his city.

So he urged the people of Miletus to rebel against Persian rule and follow him to independence. Many other Greek cities along the east coast of the Aegean were electrified at the thought of freedom from foreign rule and joined his cause. Even the free cities of Athens and Eretria on the mainland of Greece gave active support to this valiant effort. The assembled Greek force was truly impressive. It marched to the Persian governor's palace at Sardis, forced him out, and burned his city. But the Persian military units regrouped and counter-attacked strongly. Over the course of six years the Persians managed to rout the fleet of these allied cities, utterly destroy Miletus, and recapture each of the other Greek cities they previously held.

So the Persians had the satisfaction punishing all the Greek cities that had fought against them—with the exception of Athens and Eretria on the west side of the Aegean Sea. To finish that harsh task, the Persian king assembled a major force in 490 BC and came by sea to Eretria just north of Attica, where his men quickly sacked that city. Then the Persian soldiers landed at Marathon and set up camp only twenty-six miles from Athens.

Seeing this powerful foreign force preparing to march on them, the people of Athens were desperate for support. They pleaded for help from Sparta and other Greek cities, but no aid came. Standing alone, they were resolutely preparing for battle at Marathon when the small town of Plataea—which had once been helped by Athens—came to fight beside them. Though the reinforcement was small, the people of Athens learned that the Plataeans had sent every man in their town who was of fighting age. Nothing was held back. This idea so inspired the Athenians that they gave the Plataeans a place of honor in the battle lines and girded themselves for war.

Even so, there seemed to be no prayer of winning. The Athenians could marshal only 10,000 soldiers, and they faced an invasion force of about 125,000.[26] It took skillful maneuvering by Greek general Miltiades to initiate the fighting in a confined area where the superior Persian cavalry could not participate. Even though his troops were outnumbered by the Persian infantry, he attacked them with a small force in the middle of the lines and had his major forces fight on the right and left. When the Persians surged forward with little opposition in the middle of the line, the stronger Greek forces on both sides began to close in on them. Fearing for their lives, the Persians in the center raced back to their waiting boats and tried to escape, followed by the rest of their panicking forces. This course of events gave the Athenians an incredible victory.

Yet it came at a tremendous cost, with the Athenians having to bury about twenty percent of their fellow soldiers. This formed a huge mound on the battlefield which is still visible today.

It also left an indelible impression on all the Athenians who fought here and survived. These men included Xanthippus, who still had much to teach his son Pericles. Aeschylus the playwright performed his military duty on this bloody field. Alongside him were Athenian leaders who would leave their own mark— Themistocles and Aristides being among them. It was an epic moment that they and their countrymen would never forget.

Almost everyone has heard the story of how Pheidippides ran roughly twenty-six miles from Marathon to Athens with word of this exhilarating victory, then fell dead after delivering his message. As it turns out, there was such a man, and he was a running courier, but may not have carried word of victory on that day.[27] In any event, the credit fell to him and—even down to the present day—runners keep alive the memory of this victorious achievement by Athens as they run their own marathons.

It is worth noting that there was a slender thread by which these epic events sometimes hung. When the Persians first conquered Miletus and other Greek cities on the east coast of the Aegean Sea, Athens and the rest of the cities on the west coast did not begin a war in their defense. By all indications, if Athens and Eretria had taken a similar hands-off attitude when Miletus rebelled against Persia in 499 BC, the Persians would have recovered

*Fig. 12 Greek helmet from the Battle of Marathon
and the skull found inside it*

that city, punished the rebels, and that would have been the end of the matter. There was no indication that they wanted to expand their holdings at that time beyond the Greek cities on the Aegean Sea that they already held.

But when Athens and Eretria aided the Greek rebels, the Persians felt obliged to teach those two cities a lesson—and the confrontations escalated. Once Eretria was destroyed, the Athenians could have temporarily evacuated their city, as they would do at a later date. If that had happened, the Persians could very well have damaged the city, enjoyed their revenge, and gone home—with that being the end of the conflict. But instead Marathon happened. And if the Persians had been upset before, the shameful defeat at Marathon generated so much embarrassment and anger that all-out war with the Greeks—and especially with Athens—was now mandatory to recover their honor.

It was the small sparks struck when Athens aided Miletus that had become fanned into the raging flames of the Persian War.

POWER AND OSTRACISM

The incredible Greek victory at Marathon caused great honor and adulation to fall upon Athens' commanding general Miltiades. But there was much more to the man than that amazing deed. He was from the same clan as Peisistratos in the eastern part of Attica known as Philaidai, and their two families were intertwined in more ways than one. In the same year Miltiades was born, 555 BC, his uncle Miltiades-the-Elder sailed to the northeast part of the Aegean Sea and established himself as tyrant over the land known as the Thracian Chersonese. Having only a small military force under his command, he placed his land under the protection of Athens.

So the younger Miltiades not only had an uncle who was a tyrant, he grew up in Athens under Peisistratos and his tyrant son Hippias. Very much in the center of Athenian society at that time, young Miltiades even became *archon eponymos* of the city in 524 BC. This put him in excellent position to take advantage when the successor to his uncle died eight years later. Hippias, as protector of that distant city-state, naturally appointed his clansman Miltiades as the new tyrant there. So Miltiades went to that unruly land

Fig. 13 Miltiades

beside the Hellespont, gateway to the Black Sea, and established himself by imposing stern rule supported by 500 soldiers he recruited for that purpose.

Three years later, in 513 BC, he had new problems when the Persian army emerged from its base in Anatolia and crossed the Hellespont to take control of lands to the west of that waterway. Miltiades was allowed to retain his position as tyrant, but only by swearing loyalty to the Persian king. Within two years, however, Miltiades' plans to strike back at the Persians were discovered and he had to flee. So when the city of Miletus began its revolt in 499 BC, he was among the first to join the revolutionary ranks. Unfortunately the Persians quashed the rebellion, forcing him to leave that part of the Aegean Sea and return to Athens.

His reception in the now-democratic city of Athens was not warm at all. As a clansman of the disgraced Peisistratid tyrants, and a tyrant himself, he was highly distrusted. Openly opposed to him were the leaders of the Alcmaeonid family who had been the staunchest adversaries of the Athenian tyrants and led the fight to drive them out. But Miltiades presented himself as a man who had fought against the Persians and knew their tactics—which would be of great value if the Persians attacked Athens, as everyone expected. So he was allowed to return.

In 490 BC, when the foreign threat became real and the Persians landed at Marathon, it was Miltiades who was chosen to lead Athens into battle. And he acquitted himself brilliantly.

The problems he caused began immediately thereafter. Miltiades capitalized on his new-found popularity by asking for—and receiving—*carte blanche* to lead an Athenian force against a target of his choosing. This was the kind of authority only given to tyrants, but his opponents were helpless to stop him due to the euphoria over Marathon.

So Miltiades personally led this expedition against the island of Paros. When it failed, he sailed home injured and disgraced. His ship no sooner hit shore in Attica than his opponents went into action. Xanthippus, the father of Pericles, now stood at the head of the Alcmaeonid family and became the lead prosecutor of the case against Miltiades. Ostensibly, the charge was his guarantee to the people of Athens that the expedition would be successful, and the huge waste of public funds consumed in his folly. But the tenacity of this attack on the hero of Marathon spoke of a deep-seated fear of return to tyranny.

Xanthippus successfully pressed his case and asked for the death penalty. The jury agreed with conviction on the charges, but was swayed by the defendant's unquestioned service to the city, so they imposed a fine instead. As a compromise they decided on an amount of fifty *talents* of silver, a figure so high that he would be unable to pay it. And so Miltiades was cast into prison. Mercifully, he soon died from the severity of his wounds.

This trial sent shock waves through Athenian society when they realized how close Miltiades had come to re-establishing tyranny in their city. As a result they began to implement a new process called *ostracism*.

The practice of *ostracism* was exceedingly strange. When one hears that the people of Athens often rewarded their greatest leaders by banishing them from the city, it would seem impossible—like a mocking story made up by derisive Spartans. But undisputed evidence clearly showed that it happened many times.

Cleisthenes was credited with establishing this practice when he reformed the laws governing Athens, but he may well have designed it based on Solon's experiences many years earlier. Solon was said to have "voluntarily" left the city for ten years after implementing many laws that pleased and displeased different citizens.

> He made his ownership of a vessel an excuse for foreign travel, and set sail, after obtaining from the Athenians leave of absence for ten years. In this time he hoped they would be accustomed to his laws.
>
> Plutarch
> *Solon 25:5*

Notice that the citizens actually voted on whether Solon should leave for ten years. He was arguably the leading figure in Athens at this time, and the process of voting to send him away for that period of time clearly made a vivid impression on all living people in the city. Cleisthenes simply wrote it into law at a later date as a right of the people to exercise this authority over their leaders.

The motivation for Cleisthenes to take this step was highly evident. He had just finished driving the tyrants from Athens, after two generations of such rulers. Clearly it was better to stop potential tyrants before they could entrench themselves that deeply in power.

All of that would seem to be an excellent idea. But what kind of man would be a potential tyrant? In Athens, the prototype for such a man was Peisistratos. During the time of his rise to power he was handsome, from a good Athenian family, wealthy, a successful general, politically connected, and able to express himself well with words. He had risen to stand among the highest leaders in the city, and had many followers. With all those things working in his favor, Peisistratos was well-prepared to move into the role of tyrant, and move into it he did.

To the Athenians, then, those were the characteristics in a leader that were the most dangerous. So they kept close watch and held the weapon of *ostracism* in their hand to use against anyone who met those criteria.

The only problem was that those characteristics described most of the great Athenian leaders. And their opponents made certain the weapon was used.

One year after the trial of Miltiades, the first leader was ostracized from Athens. He was Hipparchos son of Charmos, who was said to be related to the Peisistratid family of tyrants.

Showing that this was an equal-opportunity process, in 486 BC Megacles son of Hippocrates was evicted, even though he was a member of the Alcmaeonid family. He may not have been as powerful as his brother-in-law Xanthippus, but words written on the pottery ballots cast against him suggested he had also incurred some degree of public contempt.[28]

How powerful had Xanthippus become by this time? In 484 BC another vote was held. He was *ostracized* from the city of Athens, without having done anything more improper than to acquire too much influence and authority.

Fig. 14 One of the ostraka votes cast against Xanthippus (top, seen close up) along with a collection of ostraka votes cast in various years.

At this time Pericles was eleven years of age—just old enough to understand what was happening. And he was old enough to miss his friends and home when he and his family went with their father into banishment. The memory of being cast out of Athens at the whim of the public would affect many things Pericles did during the rest of his life.

Yet even as those leadership struggles went on, the city of Athens faced other serious dangers as well, not the least of which came from the Persians. The inglorious manner in which that foreign adversary had been forced from the field virtually guaranteed their return in larger numbers.

Fortunately, the gods were on the side of Athens. The Persian army was delayed when their king, Darius the Great, died and the crown passed to his son Xerxes. The new ruler then had to put down revolts in Egypt and Babylonia before he could complete the preparations his father had started for a grand force to defeat the Greeks.

This gave Athens time to prepare. And a rising star named Themistocles labored harder than anyone else to make his city ready for the coming confrontation. Born in 524 BC to a family of modest means, Themistocles worked his way upward in politics by courting the poorer members of Athenian society—who happened to make up the largest bloc of voters. At only thirty-one years of age he was elected[29] to the highest office in the city, that of *archon eponymos*.

After the *ostracism* of Xanthippus, Themistocles bravely stepped into the void that was left in Athenian politics. His driving compulsion was to prepare for the expected return of the Persians, and it was a message that resonated with his countrymen. During his one year as *archon* he had started work on fortifying a new port called Piraeus southwest of Athens, and now he returned to that task with a sense of urgency.

Up until that time the people of Athens had always used the closest point on the Mediterranean shore as their port, three miles due south of the city. This was a marshy area called Phaleron. Themistocles promised that the nearby rocky area around Piraeus

Fig. 15 Themistocles

would be able to handle many more ships and was a much more defensible position in these perilous times.

While his work on building defensive walls at Piraeus slowly went ahead, Themistocles also labored to increase the number of navy ships.

Good fortune aided him in this endeavor because a huge vein of silver was discovered at this time near the existing mines in Laurion on the southern tip of Attica.[30] The city of Athens received a windfall of one hundred *talents* of silver from this, and he proposed using all of it to build war ships that would give Athens a full-sized navy to protect itself.

But a formidable opponent named Aristides arose and argued that the money should be distributed to the people of Athens—a very attractive idea. Aristides came from a family of modest means, just as Themistocles had done, but being six years older Aristides had won a post as one of the generals at Marathon. After the war, it happened that Aristides was chosen to be *archon eponymos* the following year. But unlike Themistocles' alignment with the poorer people of the city, Aristides favored the great families and the middle class. That made the two men distinct rivals on almost every issue.

In the case of the war ships, building a navy would directly benefit the poorer citizens by giving them gainful employment in the construction work, and later—when the ships were completed—in the rowing of those ships. But members of the middle class feared a large navy might draw attention and possibly glory away from the *hoplite* infantry soldiers upon which the city had always relied. In those days it was a defining characteristic of the middle class that they had enough resources to equip themselves in *hoplite* armor and weaponry. And they took intense pride in performing this role. Their importance to the city was reaffirmed by the essential role they recently played at Marathon. And Themistocles wanted to build a navy? Atristides would have none of it.

Yet Themistocles skillfully prevailed, and won approval for one hundred war ships to be built.[31] These powerful *triremes* had three banks of oars for speed and maneuverability, and would become critical in the coming struggles with Persia. Even so, Aristides continued to oppose him. So the two men actively campaigned to get the other one *ostracized* from the city. Around 482 BC Themistocles won this political wrestling match with Aristides and had the man *ostracized*.

So the preparations for war went ahead unabated. And it was fortunate that they did, for the Persians were already amassing their armies and the invasion was imminent.

VICTORY AT SEA, DESTRUCTION ON LAND

King Xerxes of the Persians gave up the element of surprise, if he had any, by sending messengers to all the Greek cities except Athens and Sparta demanding gifts of earth and water—and telling them to be ready to provide food to the king when he came.[32] He seemed to be sure Athens and Sparta would not bow down, but hoped to flush out some defectors and divide the Greeks. Instead he accomplished the opposite result. Representatives from many Greek cities quickly met in Corinth and formed an alliance against the coming invasion. With the threat of war now clearly at their door, the people of Athens voted to build even more war ships than they had authorized before. And the few men who had been *ostracized* were promptly recalled. Some of them, like Xanthippus, were generals and would be needed.

In 480 BC the massive army of Xerxes crossed the Hellespont from Anatolia into Northern Greece and began its march of conquest. The Persian fleet was said to contain 600 to 1,200 ships, and it moved along the shore in step with the army. Xerxes' ground troops were variously reported to be 100,000 to a million men.

With that large a force they marched unopposed through all the northern lands.

Themistocles urged the Greeks to use the lessons of Marathon and find a restricted space to fight—one where the overwhelming numbers in the Persian army would be of little benefit. In particular, he proposed blocking the pass at Thermopylae with Greek troops. To prevent the Persian navy from coming to the aid of its soldiers, he also recommended using Greek ships to block the Strait of Artemision between the mainland and the large island of Euboea. Having no better plan, the Greek allies agreed. They chose the Spartans to lead the land forces and the Athenians to lead the naval force. The people of Athens, fearing that the Persians might not be turned back, evacuated their women and children to the town of Troezen in the Peloponnesus.

When the Persians arrived, the Greeks confronted them at the narrowest part of the pass at Thermopylae. For two days they defeated every Persian force sent against them. But finally a local resident betrayed them and told the Persians of a mountain path that went around the pass. So the invaders sent troops that way to attack the Greeks from behind. Learning of those plans, King Leonidas of Sparta ordered the allied troops to retreat, but stayed himself with a smaller body of 300 Spartans and a few other men, determined to fight on and allow the others to escape. On the third day, he and all his men died in battle at the pass of Thermopylae. It was a moment that would long be remembered.

Meanwhile the Athenian-led fleet of 271 ships had successfully used the narrow waterway to keep the Persian fleet away from the battlefield. But now that the Greek armies were pulling back, their navy did also. Sailing quickly to Athens they evacuated the last of the citizens from the city to the nearby island of Salamis. Then they arrayed their ships in front of that island for a final stand.

Xerxes' troops marched southward from Thermopylae and easily occupied Delphi and Thebes. Then they pressed on to Athens where they encountered only a few die-hards who had barricaded themselves on the Acropolis. Sweeping through the city, Xerxes ordered Athens—which had been a thorn in the hand of Persia for nineteen years—to be leveled. And so it was done.

Fig. 16 King Leonidas and the Spartans
before the final battle of Thermopylae

The Old Temple of Athena was devastated, as were the upper parts of the Pelasgian wall around the Acropolis. The Royal Stoa and other buildings in the Agora were torn down, as well as homes and walls throughout the city. Herodotus told us that the Persian commander....

> ....put Athens to the torch and tore down any remaining upright bits of city wall, house, or shrine, until they were all just rubble.[33]

But at least the people of Athens were still safe at Salamis and Troezen. And the Greek navy stood between them and the Persians.

Themistocles became the effective leader of the Greek navy, and kept all his ships—which now numbered 310—in the narrow straits between Salamis and the mainland. Xerxes, anxious to destroy the fleet so he could complete his victory, sent an overwhelming force of 600 to 800 ships into the straits. Yet once again, the Greeks were better able to maneuver in close quarters—and the Persians were soundly defeated.

With winter coming on, Xerxes accepted that he had done all he could do at this time and withdrew his troops. He left a significant force under his general Mardonius in Boeotia and Thessaly, but took the majority of his troops with him back to the Persian empire.

With the Persians out of Attica, the people of Athens returned to their burned-out homes and temples, and set about trying to repair what had been done.

Yet the fighting was not over. In the spring of 479 BC the Persians tried to split the Greek forces by offering a separate peace to Athens. But the Athenians refused that offer, then evacuated all their citizens to Salamis again, knowing what would happen next. It was no surprise at all when Mardonius marched south with his Persian forces and re-took Athens. He immediately destroyed whatever repairs had been made and any structures that had been missed the first time. The desolation of the city was absolute.

Even so, no aid came from Sparta. So the leaders of Athens, Plataea and the nearby city of Megara sent an ultimatum to the

*Fig. 17 Greek hoplite soldier fights a Persian in this
picture from the bottom of a kylix drinking cup*

Spartans. Either Sparta would come join this fight north of the Peloponnesus or those cities would all surrender to the Persians. That would leave Sparta and its few remaining allies to fight the Persians by themselves. With that undesirable prospect in view, Sparta finally marched northward and joined the other Greeks. That led to the Battle of Plataea, where the Greeks routed the Persians and broke the back of the Persian invasion.

While that battle was still raging, Xanthippus took the remaining Greek fleet and went in pursuit of the retreating Persian navy. He learned that they had retreated to the island of Samos on the eastern side of the Aegean Sea, and set sail with all haste.

The leaders of the Persian fleet discovered the assault was coming, and tried to learn from their defeat at sea beside Salamis. They changed the dynamics of the fight by sailing the short distance to the mainland and beaching their ships at the foot of Mount Mycale, not far from Miletus. There they fortified the surrounding area, which would force any arriving Greeks to come ashore and face them in a land battle. When Xanthippus' fleet came in view, they got their wish. The ships disgorged their Athenian and Spartan troops who surged forward and attacked the Persian lines. On that day the fighting favored the Greeks, and Xanthippus was victorious. The captured ships—all that remained of the Persian fleet—were burned to ashes.

With that final battle the Persian invasion was brought to a halt. The Greeks had done the seemingly impossible and prevailed against vastly greater numbers of foreign troops on land and at sea. Other confrontations would follow over the years, but the Persians never again came farther west than the lands they held at that moment.

And yet all the battles fought up to this point had been on Greek soil. Vast amounts of destruction had been wrought which now needed to be repaired. This was especially true of Athens, which had been devastated. Even so, her most important resource—her people—had survived. And spirits were high after the stunning victories on land and sea.

While Xanthippus was savoring his great victory in battle against the Persians, there was no way for him to know that one of his greatest claims to fame was not there on the beach, but rather was waiting for him at home. Because that is where his son Pericles was at that moment. Just sixteen years of age, the lad was helping to sort through the debris of Athens and build the protective walls that it desperately needed.

> The Athenians began with great enthusiasm to build the walls, sparing neither houses nor tombs. And everyone joined in the task, both children and women and, in a word, every alien and slave, no one of them showing any lack of zeal.
>
> Diodorus 11:40

Nor was that work alongside other citizens the only education Pericles was receiving. Contrary to what one might expect, it was not easy growing up the son of a famous general and a woman from the renowned Alcmaeonid family.

His father's successes on the field of battle and fortunate marriage into one of the city's most influential families had painted a target on his back, a point brought home with great impact several years earlier when Xanthippus was ostracized from Athens. The eleven-year-old Pericles had been forced to face that feeling of rejection as he walked out of Athens with his family. He was told that exile would last ten years, which meant the most important moment of his life—being accepted into the city on his eighteenth birthday as an adult citizen—was not going to happen, or would be delayed indefinitely. That was the case because this coming-of-age ritual required him to physically appear in the *deme* or community into which he was born—with his father alongside as sponsor—and be accepted by the men of the *deme*. But due to the banishment they could not enter Athens to do this.

So for four years Pericles lived in exile. Then came the joyful recall of Xanthippus and his family to Athens. Pericles returned with them to the city, but could be excused if he retained a sense of dread that some other public whim might send them away again.

During the next two years of all-out war, Pericles was too young to fight so he was believed to be among those sent to the island of Salamis with the responsibility of looking after his mother and the rest of their household. When the fighting finally ended, he would have brought them back to the still-smoking Athens and what remained of their home.

His father's service as a general in the final, decisive battle of that war won over the affection of the people of Athens again. And as his home and city began to recover some semblance of their former existence, the wounds began to heal.

But the pain of exile left a lasting mark on young Pericles. What had happened to his father could just as easily happen to him. His family's prominence and the public's fear of tyranny were things he could not change. To make matters worse, fickle fate had given him a physical appearance similar to the tyrant Peisistratos. The Greek historian Plutarch gave us this look inside Pericles' life.

> As a young man, Pericles was exceedingly reluctant to face the people, since it was thought that in feature he was like the tyrant Peisistratus; and when men well on in years remarked also that his voice was sweet, and his tongue glib and speedy in discourse, they were struck with amazement at the resemblance. Besides, since he was rich, of brilliant lineage, and had friends of the greatest influence, he feared that he might be *ostracized*, and so at first had naught to do with politics….[34]

The way young Pericles dealt with these pressures was to fully devote himself to his studies.

> His teacher in music, most writers state, was Damon…but Aristotle says he had a thorough musical training at the hands of Pythocleides. Now Damon seems to have been a consummate sophist [a paid teacher of philosophy and rhetoric], but to have taken refuge behind the name of music in order to conceal from the multitude his real power, and he associated with Pericles, that political athlete, as it were, in the capacity of rubber and trainer. However, Damon was

Fig. 18 Anaxagoras

not left unmolested in this use of his lyre as a screen, but was *ostracized* for being a great schemer and a friend of tyranny, and became a butt of the comic poets…. Pericles was also a pupil of Zeno the Eleatic, who discoursed on the natural world….

But the man who most consorted with Pericles, and did most to clothe him with a majestic demeanour that had more weight than any demagogue's appeals, yes, and who lifted on high and exalted the dignity of his character, was Anaxagoras the Clazomenian, whom men of that day used to call "Nous," either because they admired that comprehension of his, which proved of such surpassing greatness in the investigation of nature; or because he was the first to enthrone in the universe, not Chance, nor yet Necessity, as the source of its orderly arrangement, but Mind (Nous) pure and simple, which distinguishes and sets apart, in the midst of an otherwise chaotic mass, the substances which have like elements.

This man Pericles extravagantly admired, and being gradually filled full of the so-called higher philosophy and elevated speculation, he not only had, as it seems, a spirit that was solemn and a discourse that was lofty and free from plebeian and reckless effrontery, but also a composure of countenance that never relaxed into laughter, a gentleness of carriage and cast of attire that suffered no emotion to disturb it while he was speaking, a modulation of voice that was far from boisterous, and many similar characteristics which struck all his hearers with wondering amazement.

Plutarch
Pericles 4-6

Two years after the war ended, Pericles went with his father to their *deme* of Cholargos, which was located north of the city walls. This was the district where their family estate was located and where generations of their family had been born. There the lad was accepted by the other men of the *deme* and, surrounded by them, became an adult citizen of Athens.[35]

Another part of growing up and becoming a young man in Athens was learning the rules of the game with regards to sex and appropriate partners. People were much more open to public nudity and sex in ancient Greece than in modern times. But that did not mean there were no rules or activities that could shock members of society.

One of the clearest rules was that every step should be taken to protect women from advances by anyone but her husband. Boys and girls did not play together, women "covered up" to some degree when in public, and houses were built so that windows afforded little opportunity for passers-by to see the women inside.

Women getting married for the first time were expected—but not required—to be virgins. This was aided by the fact that most women from good families were married when they were around fifteen years of age. And all of these marriages were arranged by the woman's parents or legal guardians on her behalf. Men entered into marriage at a much older age, usually when they were about thirty, well-established, and able to take on the obligation of supporting a wife and household.

But there was a drastic difference in the views of people in those times with regard to marriage compared to today. A wife was primarily expected to give birth to heirs for her well-to-do husband and manage the operation of his household. He had to get her pregnant to produce those heirs. Beyond that, the husband and wife went down two different paths with regard to sex.

The married woman's children were assumed to be the children of her husband and therefore eligible to inherit from him. So she could not have sex outside of her marriage. Her husband on the other hand, faced no such restriction. As long as he did his duty to sire children by her and pay for the upkeep of the household, he was free to engage in outside sexual activity. As unfair as that may seem, it was simply society as it existed in those days.

This was clearly seen in the most prestigious private social event in the city, the symposium, which was for husbands and bachelors only. That was not to say that there were no women

*Fig. 19 A prostitute is paid for sex
on this wine vessel circa 430 BC.*

present at these luxurious dinners. After the plates were taken away and the serious wine-drinking began, the men looked forward to being entertained. Some of the women brought in for this purpose were low-class *porna* who were expected to be attractive and have sex with one or more of the guests. Separately, there might be one or two higher-class women who were trained as *hetaira* to provide a much more sophisticated level of entertainment. These *hetaira* were usually well-educated, could play musical instruments, and were able to engage the men in witty conversation about current events. One could not necessarily expect to have sex with a *hetaira*, but it could happen. And of course each *hetaira* was compensated at a vastly higher rate than a *porna*.

Nor was there any social disgrace associated with these sexual practices at that time. It was discussed openly and not only accepted but expected.

> Hetairae we keep for pleasure, concubines for daily attendance upon our person, but wives for the procreation of legitimate children and to be the faithful guardians of our households.
>
> Demosthenes
> *Against Neaira 122*

One of the complaints against Pericles in later years was that he disdained the symposia and would not go. That does not mean he was a saint at all, but this was not the kind of affair he enjoyed. Other than that, it was fairly unanimously agreed that these were the kind of no-harm, no-foul public affairs in which almost all well-established men and their invited women participated.

Divorce could happen in those days, when the husband and wife were no longer happy with their life together. But in another twist, the woman was never left alone to fend for herself and her children. The male members of her family had the responsibility in such situations to find a new husband to take her in and support her. And they seem to have succeeded each time this was needed, if written records are an accurate guide. A match was found even if a close male relative had to be pressed into duty.

Once again, as in her first marriage, the woman had little to say about who her new husband would be. But she was never left out in the cold.

There was another area in which sexual preferences differed widely from our expectations today. And that had to do with adult men and underage boys. We are less certain about relationships between adult women and underage girls, since so little was written about it.[36] But relationships between men and boys were documented so casually and frequently that this clearly was an accepted practice.

In Greek culture men were supposed to be dominant, while women and children were expected to allow themselves to be dominated. It was therefore considered normal if a man wanted to have sexual relations with a boy. When the boy reached adulthood, however, he was expected at that time to become the dominant player in a relationship, and have sex with women or young boys. The only part of these relationships that was frowned upon was when a man became an adult and continued to play a submissive role with other men. That having been said, men who played a passive role often turned to prostitution and did quite well, because there apparently was great demand from male customers.

It should be mentioned that these sexual and marriage practices definitely took place among the well-established families that had individual members known to Herodotus, Plutarch and other writers. But what happened in the middle-class and lower-class families? To be honest, we don't really know. Archaeologists who have excavated small houses as well as large homes in Athens show that the less fortunate tried their best to imitate the practices of the richer families, with the same rooms set aside for women or men as their upscale neighbors.

If a rural shepherd came home from a visit to a *porna* in the nearby town, some women might allow that as accepted practice. But it would not be surprising if some women barred the door and made him sleep with the goats that night. We really don't know because no great record was kept of such local events.

However, since these practices in Athens were similar to those that took place in other Greek cities, it would seem that they were fairly universal at that time.

All of these sensitive sexual matters took place within the social world of Greece. But the outside world was still being thrown into war for one reason or another, so that often became a critical priority.

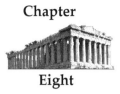
A GOLDEN DAWN

After leading his city through the recent war with Persia, Themistocles was now the fully-acknowledged leader of Athens. And he was under extreme pressure to raise those protective walls around his recovering city. Having their homes and temples sacked twice by the Persians was more than enough motivation for the local citizenry. They never wanted that to happen again. Unfortunately the jealous Spartans opposed this protective effort. Without city walls, Athens was vulnerable to Sparta's strong army, which meant the Spartans would clearly be the pre-eminent power in Greece. So Themistocles recruited the whole population of Athens to work on the walls and speed them along, as we have seen. At the same time he went to Sparta with ambassadors from Athens to delay any military interference by that rival city.

> Themistocles was summoned by the chief magistrates [of Sparta] and upbraided for the building of the walls; but he denied that there was any construction, and urged the magistrates not to believe empty rumours but to dispatch to Athens trustworthy ambas-

sadors, from whom, he assured them, they would learn the truth; and as surety for them he offered himself and the ambassadors who had accompanied him.

The Lacedaemonians [Spartans], following the advice of Themistocles, put him and his companions under guard and dispatched to Athens their most important men who were to spy out whatever matter should arouse their curiosity. But time had passed, and the Athenians had already got so far along with the construction that, when the Lacedaemonian ambassadors arrived in Athens and with denunciations and threats of violence upbraided them, the Athenians took them into custody, saying that they would release them only when the Lacedaemonians in turn should release the ambassadors who accompanied Themistocles.

In this manner the Laconians were outgeneralled and compelled to release the Athenian ambassadors in order to get back their own. And Themistocles, having by means of so clever a stratagem fortified his native land speedily and without danger, enjoyed high favour among his fellow citizens.

Diodorus 11:40

The results of those frenzied efforts are still visible today. Standing in the Agora and looking up at the north wall of the Acropolis—which was also hastily repaired at that time—one can easily see the fragments of destroyed temples that were re-used to raise the wall as quickly as possible. No attempt was made to square the stones and make a good-looking structure. The most obvious parts of this work are the short segments of round columns that make up a section of the wall.

While that critical project was going ahead at full speed, the Greek islands and other cities around the Aegean Sea were likewise taking active steps to guarantee their freedom and safety.

Miletus and Samos had supported the victorious campaign that burned those Persian ships on the nearby beach, and immediately

Fig. 20 North wall of the Acropolis with round columns
from old temples built into the wall

thereafter declared their independence from Persian domination. Xerxes had gotten no glory from fighting the Greeks, so he turned his attention to the other parts of his empire and left local affairs to his underlings. But the Persian governor in Sardis had few armed forces and no navy to support him, so he could not stop the defection of those cities. Once Miletus and Samos were free, virtually all the other Greek cities around the Aegean followed suit.

As part of this liberation movement an allied fleet of thirty ships from Athens and twenty ships from Peloponnesian cities set sail in 478 BC to free the key city of Byzantium—later known as Constantinople and then Istanbul—from the Persians. As before, the Peloponnesians were jealous of Athens' growing mastery of the seas, so they insisted on a Spartan leader for the expedition— General Pausanias. Byzantium was captured, but then Pausanias set himself up as a local lord and reportedly offered to help Xerxes against the Greek cities if he were given the Persian king's daughter in marriage. The Spartans were horrified and recalled Pausanias but were unable to convict him at trial.

In any event , the Spartans had enough of what they regarded as hopeless acts to help Greek cities on the eastern side of the Aegean Sea. In their opinion, the Persians would reconquer those cities any time they wished, so the Spartans dropped out of any further allied involvement in the Aegean region.

Athens and many other Greek cities around the Aegean Sea responded by immediately meeting at the holy island of Delos in 477 BC and creating what came to be known as the Delian League. Their purpose was to not only protect themselves against the return of the Persians, but to exact a measure of revenge by attacking Persian outposts where possible and dividing the spoils of those raids among themselves. To accomplish these things, all participants agreed to either send men and ships for this work, or pay a tax to support the campaigns.

Deeply involved in this work was Aristides, the influential Athenian who had opposed Themistocles and been *ostracized*. Just like Xanthippus, he had been recalled to Athens when war broke out and served his city well. Aristides led troops as a general at the Battle of Plataea and earned the respect of many allied cities. So when it came time to decide what contribution of ships, men or tax should be paid by all the different-sized cities, he was called upon to assign the amounts. He did this work so well that the allocations were accepted by all as being entirely fair.

Those well-received efforts by Aristides made Athenian leadership of the League even more acceptable to its members. So it was agreed that the allied fleet would be led by an Athenian general, and the up-and-coming military leader Cimon was chosen. This group of allies also decided to hold the collected taxes in the treasury at Delos. Those funds were then paid out as necessary to build new ships and cover the cost of military expeditions.

General Cimon came from a noble but controversial family because his father was the tyrant Miltiades, the victorious general at Marathon. His mother was also exceptional in that she was the daughter of the king of Thrace.[37] He unexpectedly became the head of this influential household at the age of twenty-one when his father died in prison after trial. The fine of fifty *talents* of silver that was levied upon his father then fell upon Cimon's shoulders to be paid somehow.

Fortunately Cimon had a beautiful half-sister named Elpinice who was not yet married. The wealthiest man in Athens, a gentleman known as Callias, became smitten with Elpinice and offered to pay the huge debt if she was given to him in marriage. As head of the household, Cimon promptly gave his permission. In a single stroke he not only had the large debt lifted but brought into his family a wealthy and influential ally in the political life upon which he was embarking.

While Cimon was serving as general of the Delian League fleet, Themistocles was still the well-established leader of Athens. This was not only due to the honors that the man had earned in the Persian Wars, but also to his ongoing ability to please the poorer class of voters in the city. Themistocles' major program of rebuilding the city served him well in this regard, for it gave poor and working-class citizens full employment not just in Athens but also at the ship-building dockyards of Piraeus.

The rising Cimon was more interested in supporting the interests of the great families and other well-to-do members of Athenian society. So he aligned himself with Aristides and against The-

Fig. 21 Cimon

mistocles on most issues of the day. Yet he also had to establish his military credentials if he wanted to earn respect in the city, so he applied himself with great energy to his duties leading the Delian fleet. In 475 BC Cimon led his ships against the remaining Persian fortress at Eion in Thrace, situated at the northern end of the Aegean Sea. His victory there led to similar campaigns in service to the League—and in service to Athens. That included conquering the island of Skyros and making it into an Athenian colony.

Then came the great opportunity for which he had been waiting. The people of Athens decided Themistocles had been in power long enough and chafed under his control. So they *ostracized* him in 472 BC. Since the Spartans were still angry at him for building the thick wall that encircled Athens, they sought immediately to bring him to trial on trumped-up charges. Fearing he would lose that trial, Themistocles left Greece and never again saw the land to which he had devoted his life.

His demise opened the door for Cimon, who promptly picked up the reins of power in Athens.

But even as that shift occurred, there was a younger man taking his first steps into the public arena. One who would come to play a major role in the destiny of this city.

That young man was Pericles. His well-respected father Xanthippus had passed away three years earlier, leaving Pericles and his brother Ariphron to carry on the family traditions. Ariphron took over management of the family's estate outside the walls of the city. That was fine with Pericles who chose to follow his father's military career and its more austere life.

Commanding men came easily to Pericles, thanks in part to his early education. It had given him a strong sense of how the world worked, and infused him with the calm demeanor of one who understood what was happening around him. This was evident even in his private life.

> It is, at any rate, a fact that, once on a time when he
> had been abused and insulted all day long by a certain
> lewd fellow of the baser sort, he endured it all quietly,
> though it was in the market-place, where he had ur-

gent business to transact, and towards evening went
away homewards unruffled, the fellow following
along and heaping all manner of contumely upon
him. When he was about to go in doors, it being now
dark, he ordered a servant to take a torch and escort
the fellow in safety back to his own home.

Zeno, when men called the austerity of Pericles a
mere thirst for reputation, and swollen conceit, urged
them to have some such thirst for reputation themselves, with the idea that the very assumption of no-
bility might in time produce, all unconsciously, something like an eager and habitual practice of it.

These were not the only advantages Pericles had of
his association with Anaxagoras. It appears that he
was also lifted by him above superstition, that feeling
which is produced by amazement at what happens in
regions above us. It affects those who are ignorant of
the causes of such things, and are crazed about divine
intervention, and confounded through their inexperience in this domain; whereas the doctrines of natural
philosophy remove such ignorance and inexperience,
and substitute for timorous and inflamed superstition
that unshaken reverence which is attended by a good
hope.

Plutarch
Pericles 4-6

Given his broad education, it was not too surprising that when
Pericles made his first modest foray into Athenian society at the
age of twenty-three, he did it by tapping into his family's considerable wealth to sponsor three new plays by Aeschylus. These
included *The Persians*—one of the playwright's most famous
works—which won first prize in the City Dionysia festival.

But his concerns over the possibility of *ostracism* were still with
him. So other than that one sponsorship, Pericles shunned politics
and any other form of public appearance. Instead he put all of his
energy into his military profession. And as it turned out, he was
remarkably good in that trade. He thrived in the demanding life

of a soldier and learned to work with men of all ranks on matters of life and death.

So during these days Cimon was the uncontested leader of Athenian politics. Yet it was also true that his direct involvement in city affairs was often interrupted by the need to go far from Athens on campaigns at the head of the Delian League fleet. In one of these expeditions around 470 BC, the island of Naxos went into revolt against the League, and a siege of the island was necessary to keep them in the organization. It was believed that if one island was allowed to drop out, many might drop out—making those islands and eastern cities easy targets for Persian forces. So the revolt was put down, and Naxos stayed in the League.

That was an essential victory, but Cimon's greatest campaign was probably the one which came a few years later at Eurymedon. The Persians had subjugated the people of southern Anatolia, and Cimon wanted to reverse those gains. So he brought his large fleet there and routed the Phoenician ships that were guarding the Eurymedon River for the Persians. Then he put soldiers ashore and proceeded to win a land battle against the entrenched Persian garrison. As a result of this victory, a number of other Anatolian cities joined the Delian League, including Phaselis on the shore of Lycia and the city of Knidos on the coast of Caria. It was a great triumph for Cimon and Athens.

Then in 465 BC the island of Thasos in the far north of the Aegean Sea revolted against the League. Cimon sailed there with a few ships and won a quick battle, but then had to besiege the largest town on the island for two years before final victory could be achieved.

He returned to Athens after that successful mission only to find that his long time away from the city had allowed several opponents to acquire considerable influence. And among those opponents was Pericles.

When Aristides was dead, and Themistocles in banishment, and Cimon was kept by his campaigns for the most part abroad, then at last Pericles decided to devote himself to the people, espousing the cause of

Fig. 22 Campaigns in the Aegean and Anatolia

the poor and the many instead of the few and the rich, contrary to his own nature, which was anything but popular. But he feared, as it would seem, to encounter a suspicion of aiming at tyranny, and when he saw that Cimon was very aristocratic in his sympathies, and was held in extraordinary affection by the party of the "Good and True," he began to court the favour of the multitude, thereby securing safety for himself, and power to wield against his rival.

Plutarch
Pericles 7:2-3

Pericles' initial focus on military endeavors paid off handsomely in 464 BC when he was elected to be one of the ten generals of Athens.[38] That gave him a comfortable post with solid public stature. Yet it also came with a measure of safety because he did not stand out enough to be anyone's target—there were nine other men who held the same rank. Given his family's lofty name and influence, it was reasonable for others to seek him out and ask him to join their side on civic issues of the day, but he continued to move cautiously. Even so, it seems word eventually got out that his personal sentiments were different than those of Cimon, and the political leaders who opposed Cimon took notice.

In 463 BC when Cimon returned from the battlefield, his rivals finally felt strong enough to put him on trial for his recent activities. Thasos was close to Macedonia, so it was argued that Cimon could easily have continued the battle into Macedonian territory and established Athenian control of lands there. The specific charge against him was that he did not attack Macedonia because its king had paid bribes to him.

A significant aspect of this trial was that Pericles served as one of the prosecutors against Cimon. This was a clear sign that his influence in politics was slowly ascending. And he was a logical choice for this role because his father Xanthippus had led the prosecution of Cimon's father Miltiades.

An often-repeated story told about this trial was that Cimon's sister Elpinice pleaded to Pericles on behalf of her brother, so he relented and made only a brief presentation at the trial. A different explanation could have been that Pericles was still following his well-established practice of not wanting too much public attention at this point in his life. In any event, he left the burden of proof to the other prosecutors, and they did not deliver. The accused was acquitted, but at least the discussion about removing Cimon had been started.

Cimon proceeded to dig himself into deeper trouble in 462 BC when Sparta requested help from Athens to deal with revolts by the *helots*—the lowest level of people in their society. That revolt took place in Messenia, a land that Sparta ruled. While most Athenians were reluctant to help the city that had so often tried to suppress them, Cimon very much wanted to give that support. He had long admired the Spartans and the province of Lacedaemon in which they lived. He even named one of his sons Lacedaemonius. Sparta was well aware of this, and had appointed him as their *proxenos* or ambassador to Athens. Suffice it to say that Cimon threw all his weight behind the request to aid Sparta, and so it was voted to give that support.

Cimon proudly assembled a large force of 4,000 fully-armed men and personally led them on the march southward. When they arrived in Messenia, the Spartans seemed surprised to see such a large force. That stirred worries that Athens might have a hidden agenda or a desire to cause harm in some way. So they rejected the Athenian troops and sent Cimon home in embarrassment.

Nor was that the worst news. While Cimon was away on this campaign, a man named Ephialtes—the rising leader of the pro-democracy party in Athens—mounted a campaign against the aristocratic Areopagus council. This was the main bastion of the privileged, top-level families in the city, and they were a strong source of support for Cimon. Somehow, even through all the democratic reforms of Solon and Cleisthenes, the Areopagus had kept its critical position as the body that oversaw all officeholders and conducted the state trials.

Ephialtes successfully recruited Pericles to assist him in weakening the Areopagus, and this added the luster of the Alcmaeonid family name to his cause. With Pericles on board with this effort, and other allies as well, Ephialtes pushed through a vote to strip the Areopagus of almost all its powers. With that simple change, full democracy finally came to Athens.

Immediately thereafter a vote was held and Cimon was *ostracized*. The public argument in favor of this action was the disgrace he incurred in his campaign to help Sparta. The less-publicized reason was his clear support of aristocratic rule, and the never-forgotten fact that his father had been a tyrant. When Cimon left Athens in compliance with the *ostracism* order, it was a new day for the city and the pro-democracy movement.

Ephialtes unfortunately did not live long enough to enjoy his victory. He was killed in 461 BC. The person who committed this murder was said to be Aristodicus of Tanagra,[39] but it was widely believed that the assassin had acted on behalf of outraged aristocrats.

So Pericles stepped into the shoes of Ephialtes, his martyred mentor. By so doing he became the leader of the powerful pro-democracy party which was largely drawn from the poorer and middle-income parts of the city. Yet he also had considerable support among the people of his own social strata, the great families of Athens. This combination gave him tremendous reach across all levels of Athenian society.

Pericles could not possibly have foreseen the passing of his mentor, which thrust him so quickly into this highly visible position. But there he was. So he proceeded with a measure of caution at first, applying himself to his work and not seeking the spotlight of public attention. As it turned out, this was exactly what his city needed.

He would hold this position of leadership in Athens for the next thirty-two years, which would prove to be the golden age of this legendary city. The age of Pericles had begun.

THE NEW HERO RISES

As Pericles took the reins of Athens, it was an unruly and un-broken horse he had to ride. The recent changes in democracy he helped to usher in—on top of the previous changes by Cleisthenes and Solon—left very little precedent for how the government of his city should go forward. Nominally, the most visible leader of Athens was the *archon eponymos,* with important roles being played by various magistrates. But in reality the true power was vested in other places.

The most frequently mentioned civic body in Athens was the city council or *boule*, which had 500 members in those days. These councilmen were chosen from the 139 districts or *demes* that made up the city-state. In many cases these were towns in the country-side around Athens such as Piraeus and Marathon, but in the cen-tral city itself they were simply neighborhood districts. Each *deme* had a mayor or *demarchos*, whose most important duty was to maintain the list of citizens in that *deme*. This was essential be-cause if you were on the mayor's *deme* list you could enjoy all the rights of citizenship in this important and prosperous city. If you

Fig. 23 The speaker's platform on Pnyx Hill — carved from living rock. The great orators of Athens stood here to address the multitude of Athenian people on the hillside. From a photo taken in 1865-1895.

were not on the list because you were a foreigner, woman, child or slave, you had lesser rights.

Some *demes* were much more populous than others, so they were entitled to send more councilmen. As a citizen, you could vote on civic matters at the age of twenty, but had to be at least thirty to serve as a city councilman. It was this process of selection-from-among-the-people that gave us the word democracy (*demo-kratia*).

The *demes* were then grouped together into ten tribes as noted earlier. In your tribe meeting you elected additional officers such as a *strategos* or general. That resulted in there being ten generals elected each year for a one-year term. The city then chose one top military officer or *polemarch* to lead their military actions.

The final authority of the city, however, rested in the occasional meetings of the assembly or *ecclesia.* This was made up of all the people in the city who had voting rights. Potentially this could have meant up to 40,000 people trying to meet and vote on the issues of the day.[40] In reality, not everyone showed up when these meetings were called. But since a quorum of 6000 was sometimes required in order to conduct business, it was evident that they had serious turnouts for these discussions and votes. That is why these assembly meetings were held in the open air of the Pnyx hilltop south of the Agora. The city council drafted all the bills, but as a citizen you stood in the assembly and voted on them, thus making the ultimate decisions.

The courts of the city also made some final decisions, but on a smaller case-by-case basis. Each year six thousand citizens over the age of thirty were chosen to serve as the city's jury pool. During the course of that year they could be summoned in groups of 200 for a minor trial or up to 1500 for a more serious trial.

Clearly all of this government-by-the-people required a huge time commitment from the individuals chosen as *archon, strategos,* councilman, juror and other city functions. That is why Pericles' party of pro-democracy advocates arranged for individuals serving in these positions to be compensated financially by the city. The pro-aristocracy faction vehemently opposed this, because previously—when there was no pay for service—only the wealthy could afford to hold office and perform city duties, which put more power in their hands. But the huge number of less-wealthy people in the city favored having compensation, so those proposals won easily.

As leader of the large pro-democracy faction, Pericles was able to wield considerable power on the writing of bills in the city council. He also controlled enough votes of delegates in that house to get the right bills sent to the assembly. That political power made it possible to kill bills opposed to his policies so that they were never even presented to the assembly for consideration.

In those early days it was not clear that Pericles was an accomplished orator. As we saw, he started out in life deeply reluctant to speak in public after his father was *ostracized*. Even when he was offered a platform at the trial of Cimon, he backed away and certainly did not carry the day with persuasive oratorical skills.

But as a young man and soldier he had already showed his ability to learn from mentors and from experience, and it had served him well. In time he would surpass all around him as a general, as an orator and as the leader of this great city.

Pericles seemed most comfortable right away in his military role as *strategos*, since that was where he had spent years honing his skills. He knew the tactics of siege, in which a city with strong walls could only be taken by surrounding it and cutting off all sources of food. Starvation would eventually force the otherwise-defiant city to yield. And he saw that his beloved city of Athens was vulnerable to this same method of attack. The solution was obvious—simply extend the city walls so that they ran many miles to the south and included the city's two ports of Piraeus and Phaleron.

His experience as a teenager working with other citizens of the city to build the walls of Themistocles had shown him that this was a huge project. But it also showed him that these walls could be built. The only real obstacle was Sparta.

Spartan opposition to the wall built by Themistocles around the city of Athens now flared to life again over this extension of the walls. Since Sparta was the leading land-based power in Greece, it could maintain a position of dominance only if cities such as Athens were vulnerable to attack by land. Using the force

Fig. 24 Pericles

of siege, Sparta could then cause those cities to do what they desired. If new walls were built all the way to the sea, Athens would be able to hold out indefinitely against attack simply by bringing everything they needed across the sea in boats. Pericles and the other city leaders did not want that Spartan sword—or anyone else's sword—hanging over them.

So Pericles put Athens' full resources into building those two long walls from the existing city fortifications to the two ports as quickly as possible. The problem with this decision was that it would take about four years to build these walls, during which time the Spartans would be exceedingly angry. This was one of the flames that helped to light the bonfire of the First Peloponnesian War.[41]

Athens may have added fuel to the fire by allowing the *helots* fleeing from Spartan lands after their unsuccessful revolt to settle in Naupaktos on the northern shore of the Corinthian Gulf. This was land the Athenians had recently taken for their own use and were shaping into a significant supply base on the western side of Greece.

More directly, Pericles reached an alliance with the city of Argos, the Spartans' main adversary in the Peloponnesus, which could be a critical ally in the event of a Spartan attack. He also arranged an alliance with the neighboring city-state of Megara because it sat astride the isthmus connecting the Peloponnesus to the mainland—so it could help block any advance by Spartans headed for Athens.

Clearly these new alliance partners were looking for support as well, which increased the political turmoil in this part of Greece. Megara was engaged in a border war with the powerful city-state of Corinth, so this alliance dragged Athens into that war. And Corinth was one of Sparta's closest allies. All of these things gave Sparta a wealth of reasons to go to war with Athens, and it could pick any one or all of them. But as fortune would have it, the Spartans were busy at home recovering from the rebellion of their *helots*, so any "day of reckoning" was put off for some time.

Then the people of Athens made what seemed to be a completely foolish move. In 460 BC they met in the city assembly and authorized sending 200 ships to assist Egypt in a rebellion against its Persian masters. The initial result was exactly what Pericles and other Athenians wanted. The Persian forces were defeated and driven inland from the Egyptian coast all the way to Memphis, not far from where Cairo is today. But after that, the war became bogged down. Meanwhile Sparta's allies saw the fleet of Athens weakened by the absence of 200 ships and took action.

Corinth formed an alliance with the city of Epidaurus on Argos' peninsula, and landed troops there. Not only did this action harm Argos, an ally of Athens, it also cut off the Athens-friendly city of Troezen from the rest of the peninsula. Since Troezen was the city that had sheltered many of Athens' women and children when they were evacuated prior to the Persians' first invasion in 480 BC, the Athenians now had no choice but to aid this city in its time of need.

The first campaign in this conflict ended poorly. Athens was defeated by the combined Corinthian and Epidaurian forces at the city of Halieis—which had an excellent harbor and acropolis on the south side of the Argolid peninsula and today is part of Porto Cheli. Even though Pericles was a general at this time, he was not one of those who went on this campaign.

In any event, Athens was too deeply committed in this venture to back away. So its generals immediately fought and won a sea battle near the island of Cecryphaleia—today called Agistri— between Epidaurus and the large island of Aegina. Like dominoes beginning to fall, that drew Aegina into the war due to its close relationship with Epidaurus.[42]

Many people are not aware that up to the time of the Battle of Marathon, Aegina had a large navy and was a greater sea power than Athens. In fact, eight years after Marathon, when Themistocles called upon his fellow Athenians to build one hundred ships of war, he cited the need to match the sea power of Aegina as his main argument. The icing on the cake came four years later, when Athens stood at the head of the newly-formed Delian League and took control of the combined fleets of virtually all the Greek islands. Aegina was one of the few islands that did not join the League. And now it was heavily overshadowed by the sea-power of Athens.

Fig. 25 The Argolis campaigns

here suffered a severe blow. The bulk of her army continued its retreat home.

Thucydides
*History of the Pelopon-
nesian War 1:105-106*

So Athens survived this serious threat by relying upon an army of men considered too old or too young to fight. Their failure would have let enemy troops flood into a virtually unprotected Athens. But the Athenian soldiers held their ground and won the day.

The siege of Aegina lasted four years before that island finally yielded. But yield it did, and their wealthy city with its powerful navy was forced to join the Delian League, essentially becoming a subject state to Athens.

By that point the Spartans had their house sufficiently in order to pay attention to what was happening outside their own lands. So when fighting broke out in 457 BC between one of their allies— the state of Doris—and the Athenian-allied state of Phocis, a Spartan army moved north across the Gulf of Corinth and forced Phocis to accept terms. In response, Athenian ships were quickly deployed in the Gulf of Corinth and did not allow the Spartan troops to return the way they had come. So the Spartans marched through the land of their ally Boeotia and headed straight toward Attica. If they wanted to prevent Athens from finishing their long walls to Piraeus, this was their last chance because the walls were almost complete.

The Athenians marched out in full force and met the Spartan army at the town of Tanagra just as those foreign troops were about to enter Attica. It was a furious battle and Sparta won. But in the process they suffered such severe losses that they decided not to proceed into Attica but instead marched home to recover.

Athens managed to restore its fighting force much sooner than its opponent. Only two months later it marched back and destroyed the fortified town of Tanagra. Then the Athenians pressed on and captured the lands of Boeotia, Phocis and Locris. After that, the Athenian soldiers returned home and joined Pericles in

The battles between these two maritime powers began at se.
where Athens won a major victory over the Aegina navy. The
the victors settled in to begin a long siege of the island.

While that was going on, Corinth marched a large force in th
direction of Athens, which had few soldiers left in the city due t
the other campaigns being fought. A desperate battle ensued. The
Athenian general Myronides was apparently thought to be more
seasoned than young Pericles at that early date, because he was
put in charge of the meager Athenian force available.

> Meanwhile the Corinthians and their allies occupied
> the heights of Geraneia, and marched down into the
> Megarid [the land around Megara], in the belief that,
> with a large force absent in Aegina and Egypt, Athens
> would be unable to help the Megarians without rais-
> ing the siege of Aegina.
>
> But the Athenians, instead of moving the army of
> Aegina, raised a force of the old and young men that
> had been left in the city, and marched into the Mega-
> rid under the command of Myronides. After a drawn
> battle with the Corinthians, the rival hosts parted,
> each with the impression that they had gained the vic-
> tory. The Athenians, however, if anything, had rather
> the advantage, and on the departure of the Corinthi-
> ans set up a trophy.
>
> Urged by the taunts of the elders in their city, the
> Corinthians made their preparations, and about
> twelve days afterwards came and set up their trophy
> as victors. Sallying out from Megara, the Athenians
> cut off the party that was employed in erecting the
> trophy, and engaged and defeated the rest. In the re-
> treat of the vanquished army, a considerable division,
> pressed by the pursuers and mistaking the road,
> dashed into a field on some private property, with a
> deep trench all round it, and no way out. Being ac-
> quainted with the place, the Athenians hemmed their
> front with heavy infantry and, placing the light troops
> round in a circle, stoned all who had gone in. Corinth

successfully finishing construction of the long walls from Athens to its two ports, making the city virtually unassailable.

Filled with confidence, the people of Athens sent General Tolmides and a fleet of ships to raid and plunder the entire coast of the Peloponnesus. His fleet even managed to destroy the Spartan shipyards south of that city.

Although Pericles did not march out at the head of troops in these conflicts, his judicious choices in deploying the city's forces on land and sea had borne fruit. The city walls were complete and a lull had been won in the fighting between Athens and Sparta.

But all of these campaigns put a great strain on his personal life, and things were about to change dramatically for him and for Athens.

PERICLES AND ASPASIA

As often happened with men in good families, Pericles was put into an arranged marriage when he was thirty-two years of age. For some unknown reason the woman's name was not recorded, but she was a relative of his who had previously been married to a man who no longer wanted her. So the male members of her family, which was also his family, were obliged to find a place for her—and Pericles was chosen. He did his duty and married her. She in turn did her duty and gave him two sons. But personal incompatibilities made the relationship difficult.

So they divorced when Pericles turned forty, and thereafter he lived alone.[43] He apparently had no trouble getting back into his bachelor mode, because it was not long before men in Athens began complaining that he was sleeping with their wives.[44] There were few things in the sexual realm that could shock people in those days, but this apparently was one of them.

In fairness to Pericles and his affectionate partners, however, those men had made his path very easy. They married girls who were fifteen years old and who had never had a chance to live out their romantic fantasies. Then those men left them at home to grow into their twenties and thirties while minding the children. Meanwhile the men were out on the town indulging *their* sexual fantasies. When the most powerful man in the city—who was also handsome and single—walked by and looked at these neglected women, it would have taken only a feather to knock some of them off their feet. And the fact that he *was* the most dominant man in the city left their husbands with little they could do but complain.

It should be noted that Pericles was busy with his city affairs as well. Under his guidance Athens was well on its way to replacing the houses and other buildings destroyed by the Persians twenty-three years earlier. The wall that Themistocles had quickly raised around the city's perimeter still protected it, and residences had sprung up within that enclosure like mushrooms after a rain.

The city was very serviceable, but lacked the great works befitting its rising stature on the world stage. Its temples—which in most cities were beautiful and prestigious buildings—still lay in ruins. Pericles wanted to replace that which had been lost, and not only restore the bright image of Athenian society but lift it higher than it had been before.

So he listened to the demands of the people of Athens who wanted a monumental statue of Athena raised in honor of their great victory at Marathon. For this the city had a great quantity of metal weapons and other booty taken from that battlefield. So Pericles pushed the project forward and his good friend Phidias[45] won the commission to make this statue.

Phidias was only 24 years of age at the time, but had already proved his skill by designing and casting a collection of bronze statues at Delphi. This earned him the reputation of being one of Athens' most celebrated young sculptors. Using all those skills, he now crafted a bronze Athena thirty feet high—taller than any building in the city. Then he took this creation up to the top of the Acropolis where it could be seen from anywhere in Athens. Even people on ships at sea reported seeing the upper part of this statue before they reached the harbor at Piraeus.

Consistent with the theme of Marathon and victory, this Athena was portrayed with a helmet confidently placed upon her head, a spear in her right hand and a shield standing upright

Fig. 26 Athena Promachos as shown on an Athenian amphora

against her left leg. This *Athena Promachos*, as she was called, was put in a place of honor directly in front of visitors arriving at the main entrance of the Acropolis. Part of the marble pedestal upon which she was placed in 456 BC is still visible today.[46]

The rest of the Acropolis was still largely devastated at that time, just as the Persians had left it. There was a common belief that it stood in this condition due to an oath sworn by Greek allies after the Persians had wrought their destruction at Athens and other cities. The allies pledged that the destroyed temples would not be rebuilt—so people would remember the Persians and be ready to fight again. Another good reason would have been the enormous expense of building temples at a time when restoring the simple necessities of life was such a high priority. In any event, the people of Athens were finally ready to move on, and the few wooden cult sites on the Acropolis were now joined by this towering and masterful bronze work of art that clearly marked Athens as the city of Athena.

That beautiful contribution stimulated a desire for more projects in the city—but Athens had very limited ability to pay for such public works. In 454 BC, however, Pericles found a solution to this problem.

That happened when word arrived that the rebels in Egypt—whom Athens had been supporting against the Persians—were utterly defeated in battle. That gave the Persians almost complete control of Egypt again, and freed up their troops so that the Persians could now attack Greek cities in the Aegean region once more. At least that was the excuse Pericles used to explain his next action. He summarily moved the treasury of the Delian League from the small and exposed island of Delos to the much more secure Acropolis at Athens.

In reality this change simply confirmed what had already been obvious for some time. The Delian League was no longer a group of equals—with Athens somewhat more equal than the others—who had banded together for mutual support against the Persians. It had become an Athenian empire in which many cities scattered across the Aegean Sea—and beyond—had the privilege of paying annual support and receiving whatever benefits Athens chose to give to them. It was definitely true that Athens kept Persia at bay through battles in Anatolia, Egypt and elsewhere. But not all of the cities were pleased with this arrangement.

When the treasury was suddenly moved to Athens, the city of Miletus on the eastern coast of the Aegean Sea was bold enough to stop making its payments to what was now essentially the Athenian League.[47] Athens responded by sending part of its fleet to the harbors of Miletus. Those ships and troops forced the rebellious member to pay its share and remain part of the League. Other cities took note and made sure their regular payments kept being delivered. So this union of Greek cities stayed together and remained strong.

Athens then secured its position further when the statesman Cimon returned from *ostracism* in 451 BC. Pericles put the man's close relationship with Sparta to good use by sending him as ambassador from Athens to negotiate a five-year truce between the two cities. Cimon was successful in this, and Pericles could finally turn his full attention to improving the quality of life in Athens.

One of the people who helped him with this was a remarkable woman named Aspasia. Born in that rebellious city of Miletus which had helped precipitate the Persian Wars, this beautiful and headstrong young woman grew up in a prosperous Greek family. Yet she apparently did not want to live the usual life accorded to well-born women in her society.

As noted earlier, in those days a highly-born woman was essentially "a bird in a gilded cage." Such a woman benefited greatly from the prosperity around her. But she was generally barred from any significant education, since that was reserved for the young men in her family. When she was about fifteen years of age she won a husband, and took over her husband's nice house—but also was largely confined to it. There she would bear children and live the rest of her days. Business and politics were left for the men to sort out.

Many nights she stood at the door as her husband went out to the sumptuous symposium dinner-parties where he would drink himself to distraction and have sex with a *porna* or maybe even a *hetaira*.

Fig. 27 Aspasia

Given all those things, it becomes quite understandable why a rebellious teenager named Aspasia would run away from her well-to-do family and become a *hetaira*.

Her home city of Miletus had a long tradition of philosophers discussing the affairs of the world, and Aspasia ardently made that part of her education. She became proficient enough in those discussions to later acquire a well-earned reputation for having great skill in rhetoric—the art of speaking in a beautiful, convincing and evocative manner. She soon was regarded as one of the most attractive and desirable *hetairai* of her day. This was amply demonstrated shortly after the influential Athenian leader Alcibiades became her brother-in-law.

Like many other powerful men in Athens, Alcibiades had aroused the jealousy of his fellow citizens and was *ostracized* from Athens the year after Cimon. In his subsequent travels he landed in Miletus, where he met and married Aspasia's sister.

> Alcibiades had already produced a family in Athens…. Bicknell (1982) suggests that Alcibiades married again during his exile—more specifically, he married a daughter of Axiochus, for he named his son Axiochus, a name previously unknown in Athens that remained very rare. He apparently returned to Athens with his new wife and her younger sister, Aspasia.[48]
>
> Debra Nails
> *People of Plato*

It should be noted that this Alcibiades was the grandfather of the more famous young man who would be associated with Socrates. When the ten-year period of *ostracism* expired in 450 BC, Alcibiades returned to Athens and introduced Aspasia to that fair city. Needless to say, this family link into the privileged level of Athenian society opened many doors for Aspasia. But even so, she had to be a poised and capable twenty-year-old to walk through those doors and create the kind of impression she made in Athens.

One of the men on whom she made a stunning impression was Pericles. The public actions of this powerful leader of Athens have become well known, but his personal life seems to have fallen largely into the shadows. Yet it was his personal life that drove everything he accomplished, and it was on this level that he and Aspasia connected.

He had been divorced for five years before she arrived in Athens, and during that time had sown quite a few wild oats—as many irate husbands were able to testify. Perhaps that helped him let off steam, for he appeared to have few other vices. In fact it could reasonably be said that Pericles was primarily married to his work. He even shunned most social occasions, including the popular *symposia*.

> On one street only in the city was he to be seen walking—the one which took him to the market-place and the council-chamber. Invitations to dinner, and all such friendly and familiar intercourse, he declined, so that during the long period that elapsed while he was at the head of the state, there was not a single friend to whose house he went to dine, except that when his kinsman Euryptolemus gave a wedding feast, he attended until the libations were made, and then straightway rose up and departed.
>
> Conviviality is prone to break down and overpower the haughtiest reserve, and in familiar intercourse the dignity which is assumed for appearance's sake is very hard to maintain. Whereas, in the case of true and genuine virtue, "fairest appears what most appears," and nothing in the conduct of good men is so admirable in the eyes of strangers, as their daily walk and conversation is in the eyes of those who share it.
>
> And so it was that Pericles, seeking to avoid the satiety which springs from continual intercourse, made his approaches to the people by intervals, as it were, not speaking on every question, nor addressing the people on every occasion, but offering himself like the Salaminian trireme, as Critolaüs says, for great emer-

gencies. The rest of his policy he carried out by com-
missioning his friends and other public speakers.

Plutarch
Pericles 7:4-5

Then Aspasia came to Athens, and the privacy-seeking leader
of the city took notice.

As a relative of Alcibiades, Aspasia had access to the highest
social circles in the city. And since she was an astonishingly beautiful and accomplished *hetaira,* she soon had men flocking around
her. Pericles—as was his way—dominated all the others. He was
so taken by Aspasia that it was not long before he devoted himself
to her. By all accounts they fell very much in love.

Twice a day, as they say, on going out and on coming
in from the market-place, he would salute her with a
loving kiss.

Plutarch
Pericles 24:6

Only one thing stood in the way of Pericles making his relationship with Aspasia official. That impediment was a law he had
introduced the year before she arrived.

The rising glory of Athens in those days was attracting a quickly growing population—which in turn diluted the influence of
established families in the city. So his new law limited the rights
of people from other cities. It specifically stated that a child would
not be a citizen unless both parents were citizens. This was meant
to discourage marriages between citizens and non-citizens. And
Aspasia was not a citizen. So even though Pericles and Aspasia
shared a loving relationship, as the leader of the city he felt compelled to follow the guidance of the law. So they did not marry.

Yet their devotion to each other was obvious to all. Although
Pericles had shown an inclination over the years to not attend
social affairs unless required to do so by his office, he now began
to be pulled a little in that direction. Her house became an ac-

claimed social center of the city, and her presence was sought at many civic events.

In addition to the many private affairs held by the rich and famous, Athens sponsored lavish celebrations for all of its citizens several times a year. One of the most magnificent of these was the Panathenaia festival which had grown significantly over the years.

This midsummer celebration in honor of Athena was built around a splendid procession devoted to the goddess. It included the slaughter of 100 oxen, followed by great feasting on the meat obtained thereby. And it was accompanied by many competitions of sports and the arts. Needless to say, the festival lasted for several days in order to encompass all of these activities. In 566 BC it had been decided that once every four years a greater Panathenaia would be held and be open to people from all the Greek cities. This magnified the splendor of the festivities and games. It became a much-anticipated event similar to the popular Olympic Games.

Even the prizes for these athletic competitions were truly memorable. Each victor received a specially-made *amphora* containing up to ten gallons of fine olive oil. Each of these large jars had an image of Athena on one side, while the other side showed an image of the competition for which it was awarded. Winners of the more prestigious athletic competitions were awarded several *amphorae*, with the champion in the four-horse-chariot race receiving the grand prize of 140 *amphorae*. This fine oil could be sold at a high price and serve as a rich reward for the years of work put in by the greatest athletes.

Some of these events were open to competitors from all Greek cities, and these included the footraces, boxing, wrestling, pentathlon and chariot racing. But other events were open only to Athenians and embraced local sports such as a torch race, a javelin throw on horseback, and mock combat for infantry and cavalry. There was even a race called the *apobatai* in which a man standing beside a chariot driver jumped off the moving chariot and jumped back on again. In the early days of Athens these competitions were held in the Agora. But as attendance grew and the city prospered these events were moved to the site of the great Panathenaic

Fig. 28 Prize amphora for Panathenaic footrace circa 500 BC

Stadium southeast of the city walls, where a restored version of the venue still stands today.[49]

Unlike the Olympics, there were also musical and poetry competitions. Featured instruments were the *aulus* (a flute-like instrument similar to an oboe) and the *cithara* (similar to a harp, usually with seven strings) which were either played alone or accompanied by a singer. These competitions were originally held in the city's Agora as well, before being moved to the south slope of the Acropolis where the Theatre of Dionysos was later built.

Yet the activity that overshadowed all others at the Panathenaia was the vast procession and ceremonies in which almost all the people of the city participated. This procession began at the northwestern gate into the city and followed the road known as Panathenaic Way. This broad boulevard passed through the Agora and other parts of the city before arriving at the top of the Acropolis. The centerpiece of this procession was a special *peplos* garment made by the women of Athens for the cult figure of Athena on the Acropolis. This garment was attached to a boat in place of its sail and then rolled along in the procession.

The rest of this massive parade through the streets of Athens included the *pompeis* or leaders of Athens and the other cities who contributed sacrificial animals. Then came mounted members of the cavalry (*hipparchoi*), the generals of the army (*stratêgoi*), honored elders carrying olive branches (*thallophoroi*), then men who were non-citizens carrying trays of offerings (*skaphêphoroi*). Many women of the city followed, carrying baskets (*kanêphoroi*), accompanied by the wives of non-citizens carrying water (*hydriaphoria*), and the daughters of non-citizens carrying parasols (*skiadêphoroi*). Then came the rest of the Athenian people, grouped according to the part of Athens or Attica in which they lived (their *deme*).

Sacrifices of animals were performed as part of these ceremonies on the Acropolis and at other places in the city. The centerpiece sacrifice of 100 oxen to Athena was referred to as the *hecatombe*.

How important was this Panathenaia festival to the people of Athens? In their local calendar they called the month in which the festival was held *"hecatombaion"* after the sacrifice of the bulls—and they made this the first month of their year. This was different

Fig. 29 Cavalry in the Panathenaia procession,
as shown on the marble frieze of the Parthenon

than neighboring Greek states such as Boeotia which had no month by that name, and began their calendar in mid-winter.

This impressive procession of the Panathenaia was so critical to the people of Athens' sense of self-identity that the magnificent Parthenon on the Acropolis was built with a depiction of this annual event just above its columns—in an array that completely encircled the inner temple. This carved marble frieze was just over three feet high and an incredible 524 feet long, containing 378 figures and 245 animals.

That reflected the immeasurable importance of the Panathenaia to the people of Athens. In addition to this celebratory event and the other festivals, the municipality itself was beginning to grow into the place of beauty and arts for which it became justifiably famous.

IN THE AGORA

One of the duties Pericles reasonably performed after Aspasia came to Athens and captured his attention was to show her his city. And it *was* his city, from the high Acropolis to the massive city walls that encircled Athens.

Those solid outer walls served as a bulwark against outside forces, and was pierced by major gates which connected the city to the world beyond. The largest of these portals was the Dipylon Gate in the northwest which served as the major entrance to Athens. That made it an appropriate place for him to begin a walk with her through his city.

That gate stood astride the principal highway from all the other major Greek cities, so it was a busy thoroughfare. The neighborhood immediately around this solid entrance was Kerameikos, where the city's famous ceramic pottery had been made since antiquity. The beautiful images painted on Athenian amphorae and drinking cups were known throughout Greece, so this was a suitable welcoming area for travelers. Kerameikos was very much a working class district, with small shops displaying goods made on-site by local craftsmen. It also reasonably served weary travel-

Fig. 30 At this archway in the city wall, the Eridanos River
flowed out of Athens near the Dipylon Gate.

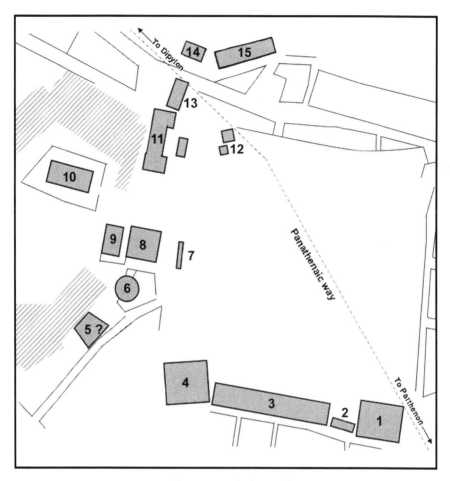

Fig. 31 The Agora of Classical Athens

Map Legend

1. Mint	**8.** Old Bouleuterion
2. Southeast Fountainhouse	**9.** New Bouleuterion
3. South Stoa	**10.** Temple of Hephaistos
4. Aiakeion	**11.** Stoa of Zeus
5. Strategeion	**12.** Altar of the Twelve Gods
6. Tholos	**13.** Royal Stoa
7. Monument of the Eponymous Heroes	**14.** Altar of Aphrodite Ourania
	15. Painted Stoa

ers with food and accommodations, and provided warehouses for arriving goods.

In the part of Kerameikos resting outside the wall could be seen the most prestigious cemetery of the city, where beautiful monuments honored many of its greatest citizens. Memorial services and visits by relatives were an ongoing activity on its hallowed grounds. Immediately south of Dipylon was a separate passageway called the Sacred Gate for funeral ceremonies and rites. This was also the place where the Eridanos River flowed out of the city. Situated between these two gates, on the inside of the city wall, was a building known as the Pompeion, where the Panathenaia procession (*pompe*) began and where meat from the 100 oxen was distributed to the citizenry during that festival.

Originating beside that building and the Dipylon Gate was the main boulevard through Athens, the Panathenaic Way. From here the city's leading man and his young guest only had to walk three blocks along that great road as it flowed in a southeast direction between the pottery shops and sundry city buildings, before they emerged into the open area known as the Agora.

This was the busy marketplace of Classical Athens, where its men frequently shopped for food and other goods for their homes. In those days it was the man's job to bring raw materials home, and his wife's job to make meals, clothing and other home necessities from what was provided.

Since the Agora was close to the center of the city and so many people came here for daily needs, the city's civic buildings were gradually built along the western and southern sides of the marketplace before being extended to the other sides as well.

As Pericles, Aspasia and others on the main boulevard entered the Agora from the northwest, they saw on the left a small but elegant altar dedicated to *Aphrodite Ourania* (Heavenly Aphrodite) and nearby there was a small temple described in ancient accounts as containing a beautiful statue of Aphrodite carved out of Parian marble by Phidias.[50]

Just to the east of that altar was the recently-completed Painted Stoa, already famous in those days for its artwork and riches. The long side of this building faced southeast toward the Acropolis and stood open to the air, adorned by a colonnade of plain Doric columns. It extended about 118 feet in length and 41 feet deep. A second series of columns along the center of the building held up the roof. Other than that, the entire structure was one long room enclosed by walls on the three remaining sides.

The paintings that gave this stoa its name were created by the renowned artist Polygnotos and his brilliant student Micon—as well as a famous representation of the Battle of Marathon by Panainos, the brother of Phidias. Trophies and booty from Athenian victories were also said to have been displayed there, producing a memorable first impression on visitors as they entered the city.

Leaving this stoa and walking southwest across Panathenaic Way, they encountered the Royal Stoa, the first building seen on the western side of the Agora. Almost sixty feet long, this civic structure had eight columns across its entrance and faced east toward the marketplace. Passing between the columns brought them into the interior, which was completely open except for four more columns supporting the ceiling. Copies of the city's law codes were kept here for ready reference. Although it was originally built around 525 BC, the Royal Stoa was largely destroyed by the Persians. Yet it was rebuilt soon after the war due to the pressing need to preserve the laws of the city. Flat on the ground in front of this building was a rectangular stone roughly three feet by ten feet, upon which city council members took their oath of office, swearing to safeguard the laws of Athens.

Further out in front of the building, and slightly to the southeast, was the Altar of the Twelve Gods. This sanctuary was partially destroyed during the invasion, and was left unrestored at this time as a memorial to what the Persians had done. The remains of a low wall were seen around the altar, tracing a square about thirty feet on a side. Openings on the west and east sides allowed a person to enter the sanctuary. This was one of the official places of refuge in the city, and no person could be harmed while he or she remained in the sanctuary. The deep reverence accorded to this site was illustrated by the fact that all distances outside the city were measured from this altar in Athens. It was considered an ancient anchor-point of the city.

About halfway down the west side of the Agora was the city hall where the city council (*boule*) met.[51] It was also the place where Pericles spent much of his time influencing the course of the city's affairs. This Bouleuterion, as the building was called, was an imposing, square structure about 77 feet on a side, with its entrance on the south side. Going into the Bouleuterion revealed an entry hall that spanned the width of the building, with a doorway straight ahead that led into the large council chamber. Stepping through that doorway left them standing on the speaker's platform, facing many rows of empty benches along the other three walls. There was more than enough seating for all 500 members of the council.

Going outdoors from the Bouleuterion, there was a round building just to the south called the Tholos. This served as living quarters for the *prytaneis* of the council. Since the reforms of Cleisthenes had resulted in each of the ten tribes or voting districts sending 50 members to the city council, the resulting 500 councilmen were too many to handle the day-to-day affairs. So each tribe was assigned one-tenth of the year (about 36 days), and during that time some of their 50 members had to be present 24 hours every day to handle city issues.[52] They also presided over the city council meetings when the whole body was called into session, which is why they were called the presidents (*prytaneis*). The Tholos was their lodging for this all-hours-of-the-day duty, with accommodations for them to sleep, eat and live there during their 36-day assignment.

As mentioned earlier, the Tholos and Bouleuterion were built on top of the ruins of older buildings that were leveled by the Persians. It has been suggested that the particular building under the Bouleuterion may have served as the earlier council meeting-place.[53] The building under the Tholos seems to have been an exceptionally large and lavish home with a regal colonnaded courtyard and two cooking pits that would have allowed it to feed a significant number of people. It was built during the time of the tyrants and—given its enormous size—may have been used as their palace.

After the tyrants were deposed, one possible use for that majestic building would have been for it to become the *prytaneion*, the place reserved for the leaders of the city. There, the eternal flame of the city would have burned, and esteemed foreign dignitaries attended formal state dinners. If that was the case, then after the building was destroyed by the Persians and the Tholos was built directly on top of it, it might have been argued that the Tholos was the new 24-hours-a-day dining facility with a constantly-burning hearth that continued the tradition of eternal flame and state dinners.

However, the existence of a separate *prytaneion* located farther to the east in the part of Athens known today as Plaka now has wide support among scholars.[54] This would have been a separate building that existed at the same time as the Tholos, which means that the eternal flame of the city would have been housed there. If the remains of this building could actually be found, that would help to firm up this integral part of Athens' legacy. This is especially true since the ancient Athenian colonies were said to have received a brand from the eternal flame in Athens' city hearth to light a similar flame in their own city, which produced a major and binding bond between the city and its colonies.

Walking southwest from the Tholos revealed an odd-shaped building traditionally called the Strategeion.[55] If that was the correct identification for the building, then this was the meeting-place of the ten Athenian generals. A legendary hero named Strategos was believed to have been buried there, and in his honor the generals of those times were called *strategos*. At this time the building was just an enclosure and rustic structure. There would be no way to know its exact form since a stone building would soon be raised there, and that newer structure is what remains today. But if the same foundation was used for both, then the old enclosure was roughly 88 feet long and 66 feet wide, with its entrance facing northeast toward the Tholos. Pericles was one of the *strategos*, so of course he knew where these meetings with the other generals took place, but he did not commit that observation to writing.

Proceeding east from that building about 180 feet, another significant structure stood on the south side of the marketplace. It was an open-air courtyard surrounded by a stone wall that was originally believed to be the Heliaia, the main courthouse of the city.[56] A simple opening in the north wall facing the Agora gave access into this 90 foot by 100 foot yard and its row of small rooms built against the south wall. As mentioned before, the 6,000 citizens called for jury duty each year were then assigned to individual trials in groups ranging from 200 to 1500, which was why a large area such as this would have been appropriate.

More recently, however, it has come to light that a sanctuary devoted to the hero Aiakos, grandfather of the famous Ajax, was dedicated beside the Agora at the same time this stone wall enclosure was built. The name Aiakeion was given to that sanctuary. There is now growing agreement that this was the actual name and use of this particular site.[57]

Continuing eastward across the southern edge of the Agora one reached the Southeast Fountainhouse which was believed to have been built by Peisistratos.[58] This building extended 60 feet long and 22 feet deep, with its wide, northern side facing the Agora. Three columns lined the entrance. If Aspasia went inside the fountainhouse, she would have been among many other women who came to obtain water for their households. The large central area had a rectangular basin of water available on the right and individual water spouts in the area to the left. Since these fixtures were connected to the city's extensive water supply and drainage system, fresh water was always arriving, and spilled water flowed out. These fountainhouses helped to make Athens a very livable city.

The Panathenaic Way, which had entered the Agora at its northwest corner and passed diagonally across the marketplace, now continued beside the fountainhouse and went out of the Agora at its southeast corner. A long-time city resident showing his city to an attentive woman would reasonably take her along this wide boulevard as it proceeded in a southerly direction and made its way up the rising slope to pass between Areopagus Hill on the right and the taller Acropolis on the left. The Areopagus was named for the god of war, Ares, who was said to have stood trial for murder on that spot. This tradition of having power over gods may explain why the powerful group of aristocrats in the city chose to call themselves the Areopagus. They may even have

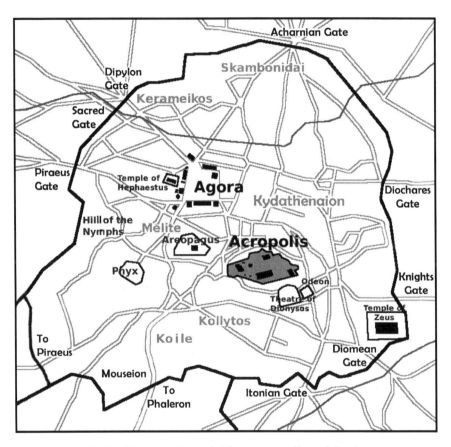

Fig. 32 Map of Classical Athens city walls and districts

met at this location to have their discussions, though several other places in the city have been named for that honor as well. Standing on top of Areopagus Hill gave a beautiful view over all of the Agora to the north.

Surrounding the Areopagus was the district of the city known as Melite,[59] which extended eastward to the Acropolis. This was one of the most ancient parts of the city, and contained water wells that had been in use since Neolithic times. It once embraced some of the most desirable housing in the city.

The nearby Acropolis was worthy of deeper consideration all by itself, and would be better served by returning to that summit in due course. For the moment, the road forward from the Areopagus beckoned, and it was an easy walk southwest along the street which now changed to several other names as it made its descent from the hill. After several blocks the meandering roadway came down to the pass between Mouseion Hill in the south and Pnyx Hill in the southwest and continued on a little farther to the gate that faced Piraeus.

The most direct road to the port passed through this gate, and that highway was protected by strong walls on both sides all the way to Piraeus. This was a point of special pride to Pericles because he had ordered the building of those long walls. And since this was the most direct route to the port, it was the most logical and safest path for travelers to follow. But given that this road arrived in the hilliest part of Athens, the road was steep in places. That was not a problem for pack animals, but for heavily-loaded wagons and people on foot there was an easier path into the city, as we will soon see.

Near the gate were steps leading upward to the top of the wall where guards would patrol this outer edge of the city in times of trouble. On other days, such as this one, a guard would stand at each gate, but the top of the wall was deserted. Knowing this, it was the perfect place for one of the city's generals to take an attractive guest. Going up the stairs to the top of the thick wall afforded a view all the way down to Piraeus on the coast, with the blue Mediterranean Sea just beyond.

Walking along that lofty pathway—protected by low guard-walls on each side—they could follow the fortification's course to the northwest past Pnyx Hill, which rose upward on the right. On the other side of the hill's crest was the famous open field that could accommodate all the voting citizens of the city, and included the speaker's platform of the *ecclesia* or assembly, around which they gathered.

Continuing past Pnyx Hill, they would come to an abrupt turn to the northeast as the wall wended its way around the Hill of the Nymphs. A little farther on, the massive wall arrived at the city's western portal, which was aptly known as Piraeus Gate.

It was on the outside of this entryway that the crowded road from the seaport arrived at Athens. By staying just west of the hills and then coming due east across the lowlands, this route was slightly longer but much easier for heavily-loaded wagons and many people traveling on foot. So this road was often filled with freighters and travelers going to and from the boats that docked in Piraeus from all over the Aegean Sea and beyond.

Walking above the busy thoroughfare, they would be able to follow the massive course of stones in a northeasterly direction through the industrial Kerameikos district before arriving at the Sacred Gate and Dipylon.

Crossing above the crowds of people on Panathenaic Way, they could continue along the wall to its northern-most point at the Acharnian Gate. South of the gate was the Skambonidai district of the city, where Aspasia's sister lived with her husband Alcibiades. This area may have been lightly settled at first, but as the civic population grew, housing started to fill this district as well.

Following the wall-top track, it began to turn in a southeastern direction and crossed the Eridanos River. The natural waterway entered the city at this point and flowed through Skambonidai before exiting at the Sacred Gate. A little farther beyond the river's entryway was the Diochares Gate, one of the main eastern passages in and out of Athens. Looking inward across the city from this vantagepoint showed the district north and east of the Acropolis known as Kydathenaion, which would later be called Plaka.

Their path along the large wall then continued due south past Knights Gate, where they could almost reach out and touch the Temple of Olympian Zeus. At that time the temple was still limited to a massive platform and the few huge columns. Neverthe-

Fig. 33 The city walls completely surrounded Athens.
This section is part of the Acropolis.

less, the whole sanctuary was considered sacred and was much admired by the citizens. Immediately south of that temple they were able to cross above the Diomean Gate which provided access to that deme just outside the wall.

Walking southwest from that point the course of the city wall progressed across the bottom of Athens. There the defensive structure came to the Itonian Gate, where citizens had access to the Ilissos River that flowed just outside the wall. Inside of this gate was the Kollytos district that extended as far as the southern flank of the Acropolis.

Continuing westward they reached a small gate that pointed in the direction of the old seaport at Phaleron, followed shortly thereafter by another southern gate. After this the elevated walkway curved around Mouseion Hill and the Koile district. This was where Pericles' elderly rival Cimon lived—along with other descendants of Miltiades, the champion of Marathon—and where some of them were buried.[60]

At that point the wall made a fairly sharp turn to the northwest and came back to the gate facing directly toward Piraeus, completing its circuit of the city. Here the stairs could be taken down to street level again. Altogether the massive fortification had traced a circle that was a mile in diameter. This meant that almost every place in Athens was within a ten or fifteen minute walk no matter where one started. It made the city feel close and familiar, and put all its local citizens within easy reach of each other.

However it should be kept in mind that many other citizens lived outside the city walls. All the people of Attica lived under the rule of Athens, from Eleusis in the west to Marathon in the east and Laurion in the south. So there were many small populations widely scattered across the land. Yet all of these towns lay within thirty miles of Athens, which meant a person in good physical condition could walk to any of them in little more than a day.

If we still imagine ourselves tagging along as Pericles and Aspasia walked through his city, we would follow them in a northeastward direction along the road that led from the Piraeus-facing gate into the city. That street wound around a bit before coming to the top of the Acropolis, where we now go.

ATHENA GUARDS THE ACROPOLIS

The Acropolis was still marked with many reminders of the utter destruction visited upon it by the Persians. The oath to not rebuild destroyed temples as a reminder of those invaders had left its lasting imprint. Damage to the stone walls lining the sides of the Acropolis were repaired by Themistocles and Cimon. But most of the plateau was left as the people of Athens found it after the foreign army was driven away. Walking up the western slope, Pericles and his winsome companion would have had to pick their way between broken stones until they reached the summit, which stood in similar state.

The one exception to that rule was the huge bronze statue of Athena which now stood gleaming in the sunlight. Since it was crafted during his administration, Pericles could proudly show it off as if it were his own. This personification of the goddess stood directly in front of the passageway through which visitors arrived at the top of the Acropolis. It loomed high above as they entered the sacred precinct.

Immediately behind her lay the remains of the Old Temple of Athena, where only three rooms survived.[61] Pericles could easily

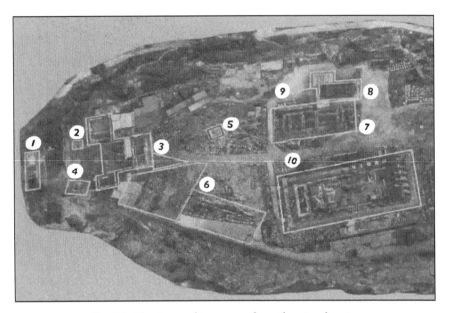

Fig. 34 The Acropolis as seen from the air, showing the major temples and other structures visible today.

Map Legend

1. West gate of 3rd century AD fortification, also known as Beule Gate.
2. Monument of Agrippa.
3. Propylaia.
4. Temple of Athena Nike.
5. Statue of Athena Promachos.
6. Sanctuary of Artemis Brauronia.
7. Old temple of Athena.
8. Erechtheion.
9. Pandroseion.
10. Parthenon.

remember this temple when it was whole and beautiful, because up to his fourteenth birthday he was able to attend observances here with his parents. The temple had been 70 feet wide and 142 feet long in those days, with six columns across the front and twelve columns along its length. Then the desecration happened.

Many people have been surprised to learn that the main entrance into this temple, just like the later Parthenon, was on the east side—that is to say on the side farthest from where visitors enter the Acropolis. That eastern half of the temple had been one large room dedicated to *Athena Polias*, or Athena as protector of the city. In earlier days that was where the figure of Athena resided, the one which was clothed in the *peplos* garment brought to her in the Panathenaia procession. The sacrificial offerings to her were performed at an altar just east of her temple entrance. But that half of the temple was entirely destroyed by the Persians, along with the columns around the temple.

That left only the three smaller rooms which made up the western half of the temple. The roof was gone and the walls were reported as being blackened by fire. So some temporary roofing had to be added when Pericles transferred the Delian League treasury to Athens in 454 BC and put it into these rooms for safe-keeping.

Moving on to the northern side of the temple, there was a special courtyard that dated back to the legendary days when Athena was chosen to be the goddess of this city. As any Athenian was able to do, Pericles could explain the mythology that went along with it. The olive tree that Athena gave to Athens was said to have sprung from the earth here. And in later years other olive trees were planted in that same place in the courtyard.[62] Also located here was the salty well donated by Poseidon in that competition. And beside it was the burial place said to contain the remains of Cecrops, the early Athenian king. In honor of his daughter Pandrosos, this sacred enclosure around Athena's olive tree was called the Pandroseion. In later days a new temple would be built on top of Cecrop's tomb and that was the Erechtheion temple that still stands today.

Among the many ruins visible on the Acropolis at that time there also needed to be some temporary structures at the eastern end for the priestesses of *Athena Polias* to continue their observances and sacrifices. Because this was the place to which the Panathenaia processions came year by year.

Leaving the Acropolis, they passed once more the tall, bronze Athena lit by streaks of sunlight. It stood amid the destruction like the first flower of spring, a harbinger of many bouquets of flowers to follow. A man in love would think of such things, even the leader of a city.

But before more could be done in Athens, there were some matters to settle with the Persians. One of the bones of contention with that Eastern power was the presence of Greeks and Persians on the island of Cyprus. That land was home to many Greek communities, yet there were also Persian garrisons that could provide staging grounds for attacks on Greek cities around the Aegean Sea. Equally as important, Cyprus was one of the richest sources of copper in the Mediterranean region, an essential ingredient in making bronze armor and weapons.

So Pericles created a new assignment for Cimon, the aging statesman. He was to lead a large Greek fleet against the Persians at Cyprus. This was a considerable honor for Cimon, so of course he accepted. And for Pericles, it was a good way to send his former rival far away from Athens while keeping him busy.

That Athenian fleet had some initial successes but then became bogged down in a siege at the city of Kition. While waiting offshore on his flagship, Cimon died from some mysterious cause. The remaining Athenian officers did not want that disturbing news to cause their Greek and Cypriot allies desert them, so no notice was given that Cimon had died. Instead the fleet broke off its siege and headed for their next objective, the city of Salamis-in-Cyprus. There they met the Persian fleet and a furious battle ensued. The Greek fleet won the day and captured many ships belonging to Persia and its allies. Still pretending to be led by Cimon, the Greeks followed up their good fortune by landing soldiers at Salamis-in-Cyprus and winning a land battle as well.

When the victorious fleet returned to Athens, a great celebration was held. Pericles quickly followed this by sending Callias, the richest man in Athens—who also enjoyed the respect of the

Persians—to negotiate the "Peace of Callias" with that empire.[63] After that agreement there was no further direct confrontation between Greeks and Persians for many years.

Freed from the onerous Persian threat that had been with them for so long, the people of Athens began to indulge more in the pleasures of life and their creative nature. Pericles and Aspasia were no exception in this regard.

In fact, speaking in an entertaining manner while in a public gathering was part of Aspasia's natural *hetaira* service. When this was combined with her exceptional education—not only as a *hetaira* but from her early exposure to philosophy—it added to her already-significant reputation in the social circles of Athens. She apparently attracted many people to salons in her home for intelligent conversation. How strong was the attraction? People came to these salons even though her home was said to be a place of prostitution.

> And so Aspasia, as some say, was held in high favour by Pericles because of her rare political wisdom. Socrates sometimes came to see her with his disciples, and his intimate friends brought their wives to her to hear her discourse, although she presided over a business that was anything but honest or even reputable, since she kept a house of young courtesans.
>
> Plutarch
> *Pericles 24:3*

This in-the-social-limelight flair by Aspasia stood in complete contrast to Pericles' desire for privacy when he was not at work. Yet even so, some of her nature may have rubbed off on him, as Kagan tells us.

> Pericles had many friends and associates…but his relationship with them was somewhat different from the ordinary practice of his contemporaries. Instead of joining them during leisure hours at the gymnasium, the dinner table, or over bowls of wine, some he met

during business hours in connection with common activities, such as politics or architectural and artistic projects, and others he engaged in philosophical conversation, his favorite diversion.[64]

It was not clear if Aspasia caused Pericles to be more outgoing and engage in these philosophical conversations. Perhaps it just happened by coincidence that he loved to do what she loved to do. But it worked for them, and that was all that mattered.

Pericles also did some notable things for the citizens of Athens. He continued to collect annual payments from the Delian League cities, since there was no way to know if the Persians would honor the peace agreement. And he brought those funds to Athens. Yet as the months went by and there were no wars to be fought with the Persians or the Spartans, it became clear those funds were not needed for more ships or to pay soldiers. So he started using that hoard of gold to transform Athens and raise it to a new level of beauty, fine arts and social accomplishment.

Craftsmen in the prosperous Kerameikos district had been clamoring for a temple to replace their rustic sanctuary on top of the small hill just west of the Agora. When it became clear that a temple in that place would be highly visible to people arriving in Athens through the nearby Dipylon Gate—and fit in nicely with Pericles' desire to increase the glory and beauty of his city—the work was quickly approved in 449 BC.

Mindful of the desire for greater beauty and splendor, it was ordered that the new temple be built entirely of flawless white marble. The temple was laid out to face east toward the Agora and stood on a platform 45 feet wide and 104 feet long. Six columns were set across the front and 13 columns on the longer side. Inside this temple was a *cella* dedicated to Hephaistos, the god of craftsmen and blacksmiths.

This triggered so much excitement to build new temples that a number of major projects were quickly approved in the city shortly thereafter. The impact of this on the Temple of Hephaistos was that resources were stretched and it took about thirty years to complete the work. Yet perhaps that gave them enough time to

Fig. 35 Temple of Hephaistos

Fig. 36 Herodotus

get every detail right. Because through expert craftsmanship and good fortune this temple has survived to the present day in excellent condition. It still stands on that small hill and is seen from everywhere in the Agora.

Then in 447 BC a distinguished visitor arrived at Athens. He was gathering material for an extensive book on the history of the Greek people, and his name was Herodotus. At that time he was about 37 years old and had already seen much of the known world. Born in the Greek city of Halicarnassus on the eastern shore of the Aegean Sea about 35 miles southeast of Miletus, he was still in his twenties when he began to travel and collect the material that filled his *Histories*. He talked with knowledgeable people in Egypt, then Tyre in the Phoenician land that would become known as Lebanon. He even traveled as far as Babylon before turning northward to the Black Sea. He then returned to explore Macedonia and many of the Greek islands.

By the time Herodotus reached Athens he had a vast repertoire of stories and histories from all these places. He used them to deliver spell-binding talks in public, for which he was well compensated. The people of Athens even voted an award of ten *talents* of silver—a small fortune in those days—to reward him for contributing to the intellectual life of the city. Seeing the public enthusiasm for his entertaining historical accounts, he devoted the rest of his life to compiling all his stories and notes into a formal book to preserve them for posterity.[65]

That Herodotus loved Athens does not seem to be in doubt. He even applied for Athenian citizenship. However that was an extremely difficult prize to win in those days, requiring two separate votes by the people of the city, so he was not awarded citizenship.[66] That may have led to some hurt feelings, because in 443 BC he voluntarily joined an expedition sent out by Pericles to establish a new Greek colony at Thurii on the southern end of Italy. This town was built on the site of Sybaris, a Greek city so renowned for its luxury that the word *sybaritic* still means opulent excess and outrageous pleasure-seeking. But jealous neighbors had destroyed that city, so new colonists were needed.

At that legendary place Herodotus continued to write his masterful *Histories* and established his reputation as the Father of History. Then in 425 BC he finally laid down his pen for the last time.

In the same year Herodotus arrived in Athens—447 BC—the people of this quickly-growing city felt rich enough to begin creating what they wanted most—a new temple for Athena on the Acropolis. This iconic creation would come to symbolize everything they were, and it would stand for thousands of years. This temple was called the Parthenon.

The Athenian people still respected their agreement with other Greek cities to not rebuild temples destroyed by the Persians, but that did not mean they could not build a temple in a new location. So they had several times tried to start building anew in the part of the Acropolis south of the old, ruined temple of Athena. But each time something came up, whether it was not enough money or not enough resolve. And each attempt had collapsed.

But now Pericles set out to do what no one else had been able to accomplish—and he was not a man who could be easily turned away from what he wanted. He was pleased with what his friend Phidias had created in the monumental bronze Athena, so he put the man in charge of all projects on the Acropolis. The task of building the Parthenon was specifically given to Phidias with the authority to employ architects and builders to make it a reality.

With that mandate in hand, Phidias prepared a new foundation south of the old temple. And on it he began to raise a structure much larger than the one it was replacing. At 100 feet wide and 228 feet long, his Parthenon was adorned with eight columns across the front and seventeen columns on its long side. At the eastern entrance to the temple a beautiful tableau was carved in marble on the triangular area just below the roof. This pediment showed the moment of Athena's birth, when she sprang full-grown from the forehead of Zeus and was already dressed in armor. Other gods were arrayed around them to witness this divine event.

Passing between the freshly-cut columns of the Parthenon while it was being built revealed an inner row of six more columns that stood before the main room or *cella* of the temple. Look-

Fig. 37 The Parthenon

ing up, one could see the carved marble representation of the Panathenaia procession that was described earlier. This three-foot high procession in all its detail and glory went completely around the Parthenon.

Walking across the polished white-marble floor, one stepped between the inner columns and could push back two huge doors to reveal the main hall. Inside that vast space the walls rose almost four stories high to the roof above, which was supported by additional inner columns. But one's attention was completely drawn to the huge statue of Athena made of ivory and pure gold. She stood 38 feet high, almost to the ceiling, with her shield and the snake of the city resting beside her.[67,68] Around her ivory figure was draped a golden *peplos* gown that clung to her body as it flowed from her shoulders to the floor. And on her head was a helmet of gold. Her arms were bare and—like her face—were made of ivory. In her right hand she held a small statue of Nike, the symbol of victory, and by her side was a massive shield of pure gold.

Phidias sculpted this awe-inspiring statue himself, after contracting out most of the other work on this temple. To distinguish this new image of the goddess from his "bronze Athena" that stood outside on the Acropolis, the gigantic statue inside the temple was called the "gold Athena." Many smaller, exquisite gifts to the goddess reasonably decorated this hall as well.

To see the other chamber of the temple, one had to go out through the same eastern doorway and turn right or left, following the row of outer columns around to the western side. This "back" end of the temple likewise had six internal columns, just like the front, and another large doorway. Passing through it, one was in a room equally as wide but much shorter in length than the main hall. This back room of the temple was reserved for the rich treasury of the Delian League, and was apparently put into use just as soon as the building was completed.

Walking out through the doorway of the treasury room again, and continuing beyond the solid columns to stand a few feet from the west end of the Parthenon, one could turn and look up to see that the triangular space under the roof on this side had another intricate scene carved into the white marble. It depicted the competition between Athena and Poseidon to become the protector of the city, with the goddess shown offering her olive tree and the god of the oceans shown with his trident opening the well of salty water. Many other gods and humans were aligned on each side of them.

After being surrounded by the beauty of this new temple, one then moved away and started down the western slope of the Acropolis toward the city below. There the hustle and bustle in the thriving streets quickly swirled about on all sides. And from the bits and pieces of conversations between people passing by in those days, one could glean that Athens was starting to get embroiled in wars with its neighboring city-states once more.

Hard-fought battles with the Spartans and Athens' neighbors many years earlier had given this city around the Acropolis some much-needed security. Firm rule had been imposed upon the only two states with which it shared a border—Boeotia and Megara—and over two other northern states as well.[69] But in 446 BC a number of cities in Boeotia began to rise in revolt. The Athenians sent General Tolmides against them, but he was decisively defeated, causing the loss of not only Boeotia but also the two other northern states.

That result prompted Megara and the island of Euboea to go into open revolt as well. So this time Pericles personally led the army into Euboea.[70] Unfortunate timing brought the king of Sparta, Pleistoanax, into these affairs at that moment. He marched a large Spartan army into Attica and took up a menacing position within reach of Athens. Pericles was forced to return quickly to Attica, where he negotiated with Pleistoanax for the Spartans to leave. Some suggested that he may have bribed the Spartan king to go. But the Thirty Years' Peace that was signed by both parties soon afterwards was motivation enough, since it yielded to Sparta control over Megara and other concessions.[71]

With Athens no longer protected by a buffer of subject states around it, Pericles moved promptly to increase his city's defenses. He built a new wall from Athens to Piraeus, parallel to—and just east of—the previous wall. As a result this left a narrow corridor between the two walls, where the road from Piraeus to Athens ran safely down the middle. This officially recognized the ascendance of the relatively new port in Piraeus over the ancient port of Phaleron a few miles to the east.

That was not a surprise, because the importance of Piraeus had already been emphasized five years earlier when Pericles retained the famous architect Hippodamus of Miletus to lay out a new plan for the streets, marketplace and public buildings of that harbor town.[72] This design used the relatively new concept in Greece of laying out cities with rectangular blocks that caused streets to meet at right angles, instead of accepting the wandering streets prevalent in most ancient cities.

Since this was a busy port with huge volumes of traffic, the increased efficiency of this new design was deemed worth the effort. And Hippodamus had previously built a similar project in his native city of Miletus with great success, so confidence in him was high. That led to city approval of the new plan and it was implemented at considerable expense. But the extensive work in Piraeus appeared to have been worthwhile because Athens prospered.

PERICLES THE BOLD LEADER

The ability of orators to sway voters was often a decisive factor in how Athens' wars, projects and treaties were approved in this brash, young democracy. Yet as we saw, early in Pericles' career he shied away from that role and built a powerful position in public office by relying upon his associates to stand and speak when bills were brought to a vote in the city council and assembly.

Eventually Pericles became a great orator, so people usually assume he must have been that way his entire life. Yet it is a simple fact that during the first decade of his leadership in the city, Pericles did not make any speech or talk worth mentioning by the writers who lived during those times.

On the other hand the love of his life, Aspasia, showed no such reluctance. Being in front of people, interacting with them and fascinating them seemed to be her main purpose in life. And this did not just involve her proficiency with musical instruments, singing, and witty social banter. She enjoyed philosophy of all kinds, as we have seen. But the area of expertise in that field for which others often singled her out was her ability with rhetoric—

the art of speaking in a beautiful, convincing and evocative manner.

In the ancient Greek dialogue *Menexenus* recorded by Plato, Socrates spoke warmly of Aspasia's exceptional abilities in this regard.[73]

Socrates:

> She who is my instructor is by no means weak in the art of rhetoric; on the contrary, she has turned out many fine orators, and amongst them one who surpassed all other Greeks, Pericles, the son of Xanthippus.

Menexenus:

> Who is she? But you mean Aspasia, no doubt.

Socrates:

> I do.

Six years after Aspasia arrived in Athens and began her long relationship with Pericles, he made the first of his great orations. This occasion came during 444 BC in response to a forceful threat to his leadership by a man named Thucydides Melesias (who was not the famous historian). And this threat was exactly the one Pericles had always feared—that the people of Athens would think he was a tyrant. This Thucydides was a relative of Cimon, the man Pericles had toppled from power. And the charge was that Pericles was misappropriating money from the Delian League to fund irresponsibly expensive projects which he personally wanted—such as the Parthenon which was under construction in those days.[74]

But this time Pericles did not turn away from the challenge. Instead he stood and accepted the personal risk, offering a speech that swept up the vast crowd of people present in the city assembly. He argued strongly that as long as Athenians protected the other Greek cities from the Persians—which they clearly were doing—then they were properly earning their fees and could use the money for these projects which beautified the city and gave a

*Fig. 38 Pericles, Socrates and Aspasia discuss philosophy,
a painting by Nicolas-André Monsiau (1754-1837).*

salary to virtually every citizen. His talk was bold, beautifully written, and artfully delivered.

Clearly Pericles had undergone a significant transition from the young man who was stung by his father being *ostracized* from Athens, and who tried to not draw too much attention to himself for fear of suffering the same fate. How did this transformation happen?

It could be that he always had the skill to do this, and only needed Aspasia's moral support to overcome his younger-day concerns. Or maybe the simple passage of years could have given him that same self-confidence. Or it could be as Socrates said, that Aspasia had a direct hand in the matter. It is possible that we will never know for certain.

What we do know is that within two years of that confrontation, Pericles did what would have been unthinkable for him before. He allowed an *ostracism* vote to be held, knowing that the two people most at risk were himself and Thucydides Melesias. As it turned out, Pericles' confidence was rewarded, and his opponent was *ostracized* from the city.

The hesitant young man Pericles had once been was now completely gone. He had become the undisputed master of Athens, and would boldly hold that position for the rest of his days.

By this time he had been the leader of the city for nineteen years. That was longer than any other democratic leader of Athens had held that position. In case after case the citizens had grown to fear the power these men had gained and evicted them using the weapon of *ostracism*. It is entirely possible that his early reluctance to stand in the public spotlight and lead the fight against his opponents had saved him from that fate. Instead, he gradually built up power, but stood in the shadows and let others speak publicly in those fights. So the fickle public anger that shifted from time to time never fell on him.

The bold Pericles that we have come to know—the great orator who led his own fights—emerged most strongly in these events around 444 BC. He had always been an able general and powerful but quiet leader. Now he took his leadership role to a higher level.

It should be noted for the record that this transition in Pericles' life became visibly apparent after Aspasia's arrival. Women have been known to have that kind of effect on men. But exactly what happened between these two people beyond the romantic intimacy described by Plutarch—and the rhetoric described by Socrates—is impossible to say.

All we know for certain is that Pericles grew in confidence, gained a second wind in his life, survived the *ostracism* vote, and took an even stronger grip on the helm of his city as it sailed through its golden age.

AESCHYLUS AND THE DIONYSIA

There was one other change that happened in Pericles' life at this time. Aspasia rewarded his ardor and devotion by presenting him with a son. The lad was named after his father, and became known as "Pericles the Younger."

Having Aspasia and his new son by his side reasonably involved Pericles deeper in the popular social activities of the day, such as the city's many festivals.

Among these, the City Dionysia was clearly one of the greatest.[75] We saw how this began as a Rural Dionysia festival celebrating the grape harvest with a joyous procession, excessive drinking, erotic dancing and light plays. Then it came to Athens as the City Dionysia with the same procession, drinking and dancing, but with the writing and performing of plays made into huge productions that came to dominate the affair. And to dominate Athenian society as well. Pericles had participated distantly as a sponsor at one time, but for most people in Athens this was an intimate and personal experience.

In addition to being annual occasions for releasing inhibitions and experiencing joy, these festivals were also an unimaginable gift to us. That happened because the City Dionysia were the source of many magnificent Greek plays that survived through the millennia. You know the names of some of the great Dionysia playwrights, including Aeschylus, Sophocles, Euripides and Aristophanes. And you may recognize some of their plays such as *Oedipus Rex*, *Prometheus Bound*, and *Phoenician Women*.

At first these early productions had only one actor and a chorus to recite or sing the lines, with masks being used to portray other people. Then the plays evolved to include more actors and be less dependent on the chorus. Those first plays were produced in the Agora, then were moved to the southern hillside of the Acropolis. There the audiences sat on the sloping hill and the performers stood on the flat area below. Eventually the flat area became paved with stone, and a small structure was created behind that open area called a *skene* which could be decorated to show different locations. And so "scenes" emerged. Seating was then built into the hillside—at least at the lower levels for important guests—and this setting became known as the Theatre of Dionysos.

Prestigious awards were given to the winning playwrights, each of whom was required to write three short tragedy plays followed by an erotic and humorous satyr play to lighten the mood. Eventually comedy plays were allowed as a separate entry.[76]

If Chronos, the god of time, were to let us stand back and watch the centuries go by, we would see the three short plays become a single play in three acts. The chorus would gradually disappear and be replaced by many actors. We would see beautiful buildings being raised—called theatres—dedicated to the showing of these plays. Then the plays would be recorded on film and be shown in these buildings—causing them to be renamed "movie houses." After that these filmed performances would be broadcast into our homes to show up on televisions, then on computers and finally on cellphones.

And all of these things began with a festival marking the harvest of grapes and the making of wine on hillsides in Greece.

As the god of time walked away, we would discover ourselves back in Athens again, sitting among other Greek citizens in the

Fig. 39 Aeschylus

open air, watching the early plays unfold. That is where we would see the first of the great playwrights rise to prominence, and his name was Aeschylus.

When his earliest plays were produced in 499 BC, Aeschylus was only twenty-six years of age. He still needed some seasoning, and his plays did not win the competition. Like other Athenians, he was profoundly affected by the arrival of the Persians in his homeland in 490 BC and fought in the Greek victory at Marathon. It was six years later that his plays became good enough to win the Dionysian prize. But even then his work was interrupted for two years when the Persians sacked Athens, and while he joined in rebuilding the city. By 472 BC he created one of his most famous plays, *The Persians*, which was produced by young Pericles—his *choregos* or financial sponsor for the performance.

During the course of his life Aeschylus wrote about 89 plays, but only seven of them survive.[77] He was in Sicily at the time he died in 456 BC and, oddly enough, his tombstone did not laud his plays—which were well known in Sicily. Instead the simple marker acknowledged him as one of the heroes of Marathon.

> Beneath this stone lies Aeschylus, son of Euphori-
> on, the Athenian, who perished in the wheat-bearing
> land of Gela;
> Of his noble prowess the grove of Marathon can
> speak, and the long-haired Persian knows it well.[78]

The next great playwright to emerge was Sophocles, and his first play was produced in 468 BC when he was twenty-eight. Astonishingly enough, it won the prize for best play over an entry by the older Aeschylus. Sophocles was one of the most prolific of the ancient writers and produced a total of 123 plays, of which only seven still exist.[79] And they were particularly good plays, winning the Dionysia competition eighteen times.

Sophocles showed great versatility by also serving his city as a general for at least one year, and was credited with bringing the healing cult of Asclepios to Athens in 420 BC. He exited the stage for the last time fourteen years later, amid much praise and regard from his fellow Athenians.

Fig. 40 Sophocles

The next master of the theatre was Euripides, who was born into a dramatic setting. His parents were evacuated to the island of
Salamis when the Persians attacked Athens in 480 BC, and he was
born on that isle the same day as the decisive Greek naval victory
just offshore. His family quickly moved back to Athens to begin
raising their young prodigy, and arranged for him to be taught by
the philosopher Anaxagoras among others. Euripides submitted
plays in the Dionysia competition of 455 BC, but did not win the
top prize until fourteen years later. There were a total of 92 plays
that he completed during his life, of which 19 have survived.[80]

One of the hallmarks of his work was that Euripides chal-
lenged the customs of his times by showing compassion for vic-
tims of society, including women. This did not make him popular
among the predominantly male audiences of those days, so he
won the Dionysia prize only four times. As a result he became
somewhat reclusive in his older years. Yet that quality of compassion—combined with an exploration of the inner lives and motivations of his characters—eventually won him a wide following.
That caused many more of his plays to be performed over the
years—and passed down to us—than those of the other playwrights.

The last of the great play-crafters from the golden age of Athens was Aristophanes who jumped into the fray late and went his
own way. He did this by focusing on comedies rather than the
more prestigious tragedy plays. He also performed a valuable
service, because he and other comedy writers lampooned civic
leaders and the events of the day. As a result they presented won-
derful looks into life in Classical Athens—though of course
warped a bit by the required sense of humor. Aristophanes was
only eighteen years of age in 427 BC when he entered his first play
into the Dionysia, but even so he came in second. A total of 44
comedies sprang from his pen to paper, and we still have eleven
of them today.[81]

Since few parts of Athenian life were off limits to the wickedly
funny thrusts of comedy—saving only piety and civic pride—he
parodied many well-known figures such as Pericles, Euripides
and Socrates. Plato returned the favor—on behalf of his mentor—
in his dialogue *Symposium* by showing Aristophanes in the embar-

Fig. 41 Euripides

rassing position of being present when those mocking words were repeated to Socrates.

Reading these plays—or better yet, seeing them performed— has a way of bringing the people and times of Classical Athens to life in a magical way.

Aspasia's Influence

This may be a fitting place to raise the query what great art or power this woman [Aspasia] had, that she managed as she pleased the foremost men of the state, and afforded the philosophers occasion to discuss her in exalted terms and at great length. That she was a Milesian by birth, daughter of one Axiochus, is generally agreed....

Plutarch
Pericles 24:1-2

How did a woman who came from so far outside of Athens' traditional society manage to become one of its ultimate insiders who walked hand-in-hand with the city's undisputed leader? Aspasia not only managed to accomplish this daunting task, but did it while carrying the burden of criticisms that she was just a common prostitute.

To make matters worse, Athens had recently passed a law punishing romantic liaisons between citizens and foreigners. And the man who introduced that legislation was the same man who now

Fig. 42 Aspasia, from a painitng by Marie-Geneviève Bouliard (1794)

captured her interest. This was her impossible dream. There was no way it could happen. And yet it did.

Oddly enough, that negative law highlighted one small factor that stood in her favor. The reason why Athenian voters felt this law was needed was due to the simple fact that so many citizens preferred foreign spouses. Even among the great families in the city, this was a common practice. The mothers of outstanding Athenian leaders such as Cleisthenes, Themistocles, and Cimon were all foreign-born. And we saw Alcibiades come to the city of Miletus where he married Aspasia's sister. In a sense it was like the Prohibition laws against alcohol in the USA during the 1920s. Passing a law did not make the practice any less popular. One just had to be careful how it was handled.

And as noted, Alcibiades' position high in Athenian society also worked to her advantage. If Aspasia had arrived in the company of common citizens, she might have waited forever outside the door of Athens' high society.

She also had an unexpected advantage over other potential wives and love interests in Athens, in that she was older. If that sounds strange, consider what Athenian society was like in those days. As a general rule, the men in Athens' great families waited until their thirties when they were well-established before taking on the obligation and expense of supporting a wife and household. Athenian wives on the other hand were most often given in marriage during their mid-teens. This huge age difference greatly reinforced the social rule that men were knowledgeable and dominant, while the women were inexperienced and subservient.

In clear contrast with that, the once-divorced Pericles was in his forties when Aspasia arrived. And she was twenty. The age difference was still there, which would have been appealing to him. Yet she had five years more maturity than the average wife, combined with the skills and experience of a *hetaira*. She had the *hetaira's* attributes of being well-educated and adept at the witty give-and-take of conversation in the *symposium*. Those were attributes denied to the average woman of those days.

It would be easy to imagine a powerful man such as Pericles walking past many young, pretty wallflowers to spend his time with someone who understood what he was talking about and could even challenge him a little with things that she knew. But not challenge him too much. Her *hetaira* training had taught her when to let a man have his way so that he emerged the champion. Elpinice, the beautiful sister of Cimon, also stood up to Pericles—but not in the right way and was dismissed by him.

Even in matters of sex, a barely-teenage virgin would have brought that touch of *naiveté* that men enjoyed, but that novelty wore off. Aspasia was a more modern woman, forming sexual liaisons at a time when she already had a degree in bedroom arts, so to speak. Aspasia made her living going to parties with men, and sometimes going to bed with them. And leaving them wanting more.

In short, the obstacles in front of Aspasia when she came to Athens as an outsider were great obstacles indeed. The laws and the social rejection of women related to the sex trade were all against her. But she was a resourceful and determined woman who used her skills to the best advantage. With effort, she made the transition from social outsider to social insider, then kept going until she won the heart of the leading man in all of Athens. And by so doing she became one of the most well-connected insiders in the city.

As it turns out, her influence on Pericles was so palpable that it was noted by many writers who lived in those days. An often-told story from antiquity about the two of them was that she figuratively put on the mantle of Homer's "Helen of Troy" and personally drew Athens into war.[82]

Because Aspasia was originally from the Greek city of Miletus, she was said to be very concerned when Miletus became engaged in a fierce war with its neighbor, Samos—and her former city was losing that contest. So when Pericles decided to enter the war in support of Miletus, it was widely believed that he did so under pressure from Aspasia. The hostilities escalated and many Athenian soldiers perished, so she bore the brunt of the blame. But Pericles was an exceptional general, and under his leadership the war on behalf of Miletus was won. With that victory came a measure of forgiveness for her. But the story never went away.

Was it true? Did Aspasia push the powerful city of Athens—at the height of its glory—into battle to save the city of her birth? We

*Fig. 43 Aspasia admires the Acropolis, from a
painting by Henry Holiday in 1888.*

may never know. But it was clearly true that the influential people of Athens, who knew Pericles personally, believed her relationship and influence with him was strong enough that it could well have happened.

That was how much of an insider she had become. This young woman involved in the sex trade had sailed across the Aegean Sea to start a new life in Athens, and had been like a caterpillar on an olive leaf changing into a brilliantly-colored butterfly.

If it can be said that she achieved her impossible dream of capturing the man most responsible for creating the golden age of Athens, then it can also be said that he won one of the most remarkable women of his time.

So, what actually happened in that war between Miletus and its neighboring island of Samos in 440 BC? Both of those cities were members of the Delian League and therefore part of Athens' unofficial empire. When Miletus started losing the war and needed all the help it could get, it appealed to Athens to arbitrate a solution to the dispute.

Athens agreed to decide the issue and ordered both sides to stop fighting, but Samos refused. Apparently it hoped to gain an outright win on the field of combat. Pericles could not let his order—nor the authority of Athens—be questioned in this manner because it would set a terrible precedent.[83] So he led a fleet of 40 ships to Samos and forced it to comply. A new government was installed in Samos and a small garrison of soldiers was left there to insure the safeguarding of the peace.

Unfortunately, the previous leaders of the Samos fanned the flames of war again, and appealed to the Persians for soldiers. They then used those men to regain control of Samos. The captured Athenian troops in the garrison were turned over to the Persians as trophies. Needless to say, that did not sit well with the people of Athens.

So Pericles returned with 60 ships to attack what was now a well-prepared city. This resulted in a prolonged siege that lasted nine months. As the war dragged on, critics in Athens raised the now-famous claim that this was all being done by Pericles to please his love-interest, Aspasia.

Regardless of the reason, Athens persisted and eventually the city of Samos surrendered. It was forced to tear down its walls, agreed to replace its ruling aristocrats with a democracy, and repaid the cost of the war.

The lesson was well-learned by other cities in the League that they should not challenge Athenian authority in such matters. And the supremacy of Athens all across the Aegean Sea remained undisturbed.

STAIRWAY TO HEAVEN

In Athens, the evidence of that city's rule over the Aegean Sea continued to grow on the Acropolis. Artisans, architects and laborers completed their work building the Parthenon in 438 BC, even though decorating touches were still being added for several years thereafter. Bursting with pride over that achievement, the citizens of Athens decided to go ahead with the other critical element needed to establish their Acropolis among the wonders of the world. So at the place where one walked up the western slope to the top of that sacred precinct they would build a monumental gateway devoted to the gods, which would be called the Propylaia.

Pericles asked Phidias to undertake this project as well as his ongoing work on the Acropolis. The master designer promptly retained an architect and a huge numbers of workers to build this vast structure in white marble, decorated with bits of gray limestone. Work began in earnest the next year on the platform and six huge columns that fronted the central building, and it spread out from there.

Five years later, as work neared completion, a visitor could walk up the hillside toward the Acropolis and see not only the tall entryway looming above, but also another building on the left and one on the right, covering their whole field of vision in an expanse of white marble.

Most visitors to this city miss the simple fact that the Propylaia replaced the defensive gate that previously existed at this entry-point to the Acropolis. And that had meaning. This new collection of buildings was a beautiful and ornamental work of art. It had no battlements for soldiers to stand upon above the gate, nor other defensive features.

The reason for this change can be found in the solid walls that surrounded Athens. They were almost impossible to penetrate. Just as the Athenians had discovered at Samos, there was no way to destroy the city walls so it was necessary to lay siege and starve the city into submission. That was also why Athens had built its long walls from the city to its seaports—to insure a steady supply of food brought by boats in the event of siege.

This beautiful entrance to the Acropolis reflected that confidence in the city walls—and seemed to show a belief that the Acropolis was no longer needed as a military refuge for the city—so it could be devoted completely to religious observances.

It should be noted that about 700 years later Germanic tribes[84] would successfully manage to invade Athens, after which time a solid defensive structure was built at the foot of the slope leading up to the Acropolis. This addition was later named Beule Gate. If you stop and look at that gate, it is possible to see the remains of ancient buildings and columns which were re-used in raising that structure.

Approaching the white-marble Propylaia at the top of the slope, visitors could see several similarities to the larger Parthenon which stood behind it. Above the six tall columns was a triangular pediment, but without the intricate carvings found on the temple. Walking between the columns of the Propylaia, it was necessary to go up five steps to where the continuation of the Acropolis wall passed through this building. Five large gateways in the wall allowed visitors to reach the Acropolis itself, with the middle one being used for the Panathenaia procession. Showing

Fig. 44 Propylaia entrance to the Acropolis

Fig. 45 Brandenburg Gate in Berlin emulated the Propylaia

the honored status of this central passageway were three columns on each side of the path leading up to it. Walking through any one of the five gateways, one found the other half of the building mirrored the front half. There were another six tall columns and—passing between them to step out onto the platform of the Acropolis—one could look back and see the triangular pediment high above. That made the new Propylaia as beautiful to people leaving the Acropolis as it was to those who had arrived.

Attached to this majestic structure was a smaller building on the north side that may have been first used for ritual dining, but was soon converted into a display area for beautiful paintings appropriate to this sacred place. The similar building on the south was added for symmetry. It basically served as a hall leading to the ancient platform extending forward from the Acropolis. That platform may once have been a defensive position for soldiers on the summit to rain arrows and heavy rocks down on attacking troops trying to make their way up the steep slope. Now it was just a prominent place where another small temple would soon be added.

Walking away from the Acropolis and through the Propylaia again, the visitor once more stood at the top of the steep slope. The stone steps that cascaded down the hillside were built at various times, and it would be reasonable to say that some improvements were made to grading the slope when the Propylaia was built in order to properly present those beautiful buildings. Yet all that is known for certain is that by 52 AD a complete new set of beautiful steps had been donated to cover the entire slope.

Another addition to the original structure was a massive pedestal of gray marble just to the north of the steps. This was contributed by Eumenes II[85] in 178 BC after winning the top prize in the Panathenaic Games. The pedestal originally held a statue of him and his four-horse chariot.

In tribute to the spectacular impression all these things made on visitors to the Acropolis, a number of other buildings have been raised around the world in imitation of the Propylaia. The famous Brandenburg Gate in Berlin was built as a direct copy of its main building. And on top of Brandenburg Gate was placed the statue of a four-horse chariot—all of which can still be seen today.

While this extensive project was going on, Pericles mandated that an Odeon be built on the eastern side of the Theatre of Diony- sos. This was to serve as a place for musical concerts, as well as a rehearsal area for the performers of plays that would be presented in the Theatre. This square building was so extensive that 90 stone columns were required to hold up its wooden roof, and its outer walls measured over 200 feet on each side. There was enough room inside for many groups to practice and still have storage areas for an array of colorful costumes and props.

People at the lower end of society also played an active role in these projects and contributed to the well-being of Athens. Slaves toiled away in Athens as they did in all the Greek cities, and in the cities of many other countries during those days. They did the hard work that others did not want to do. To a large extent this was a by-product of the many wars fought by Greeks, Persians and other groups of people in those times. Men, women and chil- dren of the defeated cities were often sold into slavery to help pay the cost of these wars.

But the Greeks had rules they followed to protect their family life from being influenced too much by these outsiders. According to Herodotus, slaves at first were not allowed to be used in Greek homes. This served to make family members self-reliant by shar- ing among themselves menial household chores such as fetching water from the well.[86] Over time this rule became relaxed, but even then a slave in the household was usually limited to assisting the master in his work, or helping the lady of the house with mak- ing cloth.[87]

Many of these slaves came from foreign conquests, or were brought from foreign lands such as Anatolia, where the Persians often punished local people by selling some of them into slavery. And while slaves in Athens were an important part of the city's economic life, they largely did their work out of sight. They toiled away in significant numbers on the large crop-fields of aristocrats, although even a small landowner in the countryside might have a single slave. They cut the stones in rock quarries that produced

Fig. 46 A slave girl attending to her mistress in Athens

building blocks for the city. And most importantly, they labored in the Laurion silver mines located in the southern part of Attica. This contributed greatly to the city's wealth and made its silver coinage possible.

Yet even a slave had rights and protections in the eyes of Athenian courts. In fact, visitors from other cities apparently complained at how much confidence and back-talk they noticed from Athenian slaves. It was even possible in Athens for a slave to save up money and purchase his or her freedom. So this was a complicated relationship between those who were free and those who lived in servitude—and it played a significant role in the overall prosperity of Athens.

Life was not always fair, even for the free-born, as we will soon see.

SOCRATES FROM STONEMASON TO PHILOSOPHER

Socrates was one of the truly fascinating people in Athens who helped to shape its golden age. Yet his life has also been one of its abiding mysteries. He was born the son of a stonemason in 469 BC, and labored in that profession himself as a lad. But not much else was said of his younger days aside from a mention in the dialogue *Parmenides*. Then, many years later, he was acknowledged as having transformed himself into one of the greatest philosophers of Greece, and perhaps one of the greatest of all time. So it is reasonable to ask how this come about.

The historical record is littered with clues, so let us see what happens when we bring some of those clues together. Socrates first appeared in historical events during 432 BC at the Battle of Potidaea, an event which was documented in the dialogue *Symposium*,[88] as recorded by his student Plato.

The Battle of Potidaea was particularly significant because this was one of the sparks that ignited the Peloponnesian War. Potidaea was a town on the northern shore of the Aegean Sea that had originally been a colony of the powerful city of Corinth. But as a member of the Delian League, Potidaea had come under the control of Athens. When Corinth and Athens became adversaries, Potidaea sided with its founding city and revolted against Athens. Upon receiving this news the Athenian generals gave their usual response by sending a fleet of ships with soldiers on board to put down the rebellion.

Among those soldiers were Socrates and young Alcibiades, grandson of the Alcibiades we met earlier. After that first battle this force from Athens surrounded Potidaea and began a long siege. When Corinth appealed to Sparta for help the following year, Sparta rallied many cities in the Peloponnesus against Athens and the Peloponnesian War began.

After the siege, Socrates and Alcibiades returned home, where their adventures became known.[89]

> Whilst he was very young, Alcibiades was a soldier in the expedition against Potidaea, where Socrates lodged in the same tent with him, and stood next to him in battle. Once there happened a sharp skirmish, in which they both behaved with signal bravery; but Alcibiades receiving a wound, Socrates threw himself before him to defend him, and beyond any question saved him and his arms from the enemy, and so in all justice might have challenged [for] the prize of valor.
>
> But the generals appearing eager to adjudge the honor to Alcibiades because of his rank, Socrates, who desired to increase his thirst after glory of a noble kind, was the first to give evidence for him, and pressed them to crown him, and to decree to him the complete suit of armor.
>
> Plutarch
> *Alcibiades 7.2-3*

This connection between Socrates and Alcibiades is significant, so let us follow the younger man's story a little farther. Alcibiades, as mentioned previously, was related to Aspasia because his grandfather had married Aspasia's sister. In addition to that lineage on his father's side, the mother of young Alcibiades was from the prominent Alcmaeonid family, which meant he was related to

Fig. 47 Socrates

Pericles. When Alcibiades' father died in 447 BC, Pericles became the boy's legal guardian. Given his ties to both Pericles and Aspasia, young Alcibiades was often seen at Aspasia's house in the city. So this was a close-knit family circle. And Socrates became involved in this circle.

When Aspasia came to Athens in 450 BC, she was twenty years of age and Socrates was nineteen. She had already been exposed to philosophy in Miletus and acquired some ability in rhetoric. Socrates was a stonemason at the time, but apparently was already schooling himself in philosophy, for it was said he met two visiting philosophers from Elea and spoke with them during the same year that Aspasia arrived.[90] So these two young people shared a common interest and, after some encounter, developed a lifelong bond which many sources have confirmed.

How quickly or slowly Socrates transitioned from making his living as a stonecarver to that of a philosopher is not known. Eighteen years passed from 450 BC until he entered the historical record at Potidaea, and even then he was credited more for doing his military duty than for being a philosopher. It was not until 423 BC that Socrates became so well known in Athens as a philosopher that the playwright Aristophanes could poke fun at him and be confident that everyone in the audience already knew who Socrates was.

What benefit did he derive from his long friendship with Aspasia? We saw how she quickly won the heart of Pericles, the most powerful man in Athens, and moved into the highest social circle of the city. Her salons attracted some of the best people in Athens to participate in her intriguing discussions. It would not have been unusual for her to invite an odd-looking young friend named Socrates to her salons, who may even have stood out in those discussions. In that forum, and as a friend of the host, a working stonemason might meet people from the highest levels of Athenian society and form relationships of his own.

In later years, when Socrates had students in his charge, he did not hesitate to bring them with him to Aspasia's on-going discussions. Even so, any conclusions drawn from all of these things would have to be a matter of opinion.

Suffice it to say that Socrates was closely enough involved with the world of Pericles and Aspasia that he became a mentor to their young charge, Alcibiades. It was often pointed out that Alcibiades was in some fashion a ward of Socrates rather than a student. And the easy manner in which Socrates would go to Aspasia's house to fetch Alcibiades reflects a familiar and comfortable relationship among them. Certainly by this time Socrates had become accepted into a portion of Athens' high society.

Yet his greatest years were still in front of him. And he would continue to grow more prominent in the affairs of the city.

ELEUSINIAN MYSTERIES

A number of people discovered that having a close relationship with Pericles—the undisputed master of Athens in those days—brought privileges, but also risks. Phidias and Aspasia enjoyed his favor and were prominent themselves in Athenian society, but even so they were put on public trial in 432 BC. The charges against Aspasia claimed she was corrupting other women in the city. It was implied that she was teaching women from good families to be prostitutes—for which there was no evidence. Yet in a different sense, her accusers' charges of corrupting women had a point.

In those days the limited amount of education given to women helped to reinforce their role, which was to stay at home and leave the decision-making to the men of the family. Aspasia on the other hand was a well-educated *hetaira* who was able to hold her own in serious discussions with the men she encountered. A number of those men seemed to feel she was setting a terrible example that other women might follow. So in that sense she may well have been a "bad" influence on other women. Even so, her conduct in these matters might have been overlooked were it not for the fact that she was the lover of the most powerful man in the city.

The son she conceived with Pericles was now thirteen years of age, and able to attend his mother's trial. The sight of all this was too much for Pericles, who put aside his usual calm demeanor and leaped to the defense of the woman he loved. Plutarch recorded the event this way.

> Well then, Aspasia he begged off, by shedding copious tears at the trial, as Aeschines says, and by entreating the jurors.[91]

So the attack on Aspasia failed. Even so, the ridiculousness of the charge against her led most observers to conclude that it was not really intended as an attack on Aspasia, but more of an indirect attack on Pericles. By this time he had led Athens for almost thirty years, and some prominent citizens clearly chafed under such a long guardianship. Yet the victories and glories Pericles brought to this city made him untouchable. So the only path that could bring him pain and embarrassment was to attack people close to him.

This understanding gained additional weight when his good friend Phidias was brought to trial as well. By this time Phidias was already acknowledged as one of the greatest sculptors in ancient Greece. His bronze statues at Delphi and the monumental bronze Athena on the Acropolis had brought him early fame. Yet he also became skilled in using gold and ivory to make precious statues. We saw the Athena he made in this way, using ivory to form the head, arms and legs, with all the rest being made of gold. He fashioned a statue of Aphrodite in this manner for the city of Elis, not far from the sanctuary of Olympia, then created a gold and ivory Athena for the city of Pellene just west of Corinth.

After the triumphant accomplishment of his massive Athena in the Parthenon, it was only natural that the people of Olympia insisted that he use those same skills to create a commanding statue of Zeus for their grand temple dedicated to that deity. Phidias spent many years working on this commission, creating a powerful figure of Zeus seated on a cedar throne which was inlaid with

Fig. 48 Phidias

ebony, ivory, gold and jewels. The muscular body of Zeus was crafted of ivory and his *chiton* garment, walking staff and accessories were of gleaming gold. The result was so striking that this statue of Zeus at Olympia became one of the Seven Wonders of the Ancient World.

All of this made it even more of a head-shaking moment when men jealous of Pericles put his compatriot Phidias on trial. Related accusations were made against Pericles as well, but he was not brought to trial. Phidias, on the other hand, was charged with stealing some of the gold given by the people of Athens to make the statue of Athena in the Parthenon. Fortunately he built the statue in such a way that the gold could be removed, so it was taken down, weighed, and found to be all there.

When that attempt failed, Phidias was charged with impiety for putting images of himself and Pericles on Athena's golden shield. That verdict was pushed through, causing Phidias to be exiled from the city he had served so well.[92] He apparently returned to Olympia and his workshop in that city, living out the last two years of his life in the shadow of his golden statue of Zeus.

As a side note, one of Phidias' smallest creations was found in the 1950s when his workshop at Olympia was excavated. The discovery was a black cup bearing the inscription ΦΕΙΔΙΟΥ ΕΙΜΙ or "I belong to Phidias."

These statues of Athena and Zeus were just two examples of how the people of these times lived among the gods. Those larger-than-life figures were present in daily rituals, colorful festivals and many other unique observances. Yet among all of these practices, the Eleusinian Mysteries were believed to be the oldest and most revered of the Greek secret religious rituals.

The Mysteries extended back to those early days when the beautiful Minoan society was just beginning to rise on the island of Crete in the Aegean Sea. At that time the people of the larger islands and the mainland lived on what the land produced and had beliefs that included a bountiful mother-earth goddess. She made the land and its people fertile and brought forth new life. A wonderfully detailed fresco painted on an interior wall at Santorini prior to 1600 BC showed the mother-earth goddess receiving ceremonial gifts. The renewing of one's life and the prospect of having everlasting life were thought to be among the compelling aspects of the Mysteries that caused them to flourish for many centuries.

The Mysteries of Eleusis preserved those early practices and added to them over time. Since Eleusis was essentially a suburb of Athens, being less than 14 miles away, the people and leaders of Athens were deeply involved in these Mysteries.

When a person was accepted for initiation into this order, they experienced the first set of rituals, which were known as the Lesser Mysteries, during February.[93] The second set of rituals were the Greater Mysteries, held in September of each year.[94] But no initiate could receive both rites in the same year, so they had to wait until the following September to advance to the higher level.

Becoming a member of this order was a highly desired honor. Kings from other cities and—in later days—Roman emperors sought and received these rites and inclusion in the order.

Although the rituals were secret, a Homeric Hymn and a number of paintings preserved the mythology involved in them. The earth-mother goddess, known as Demeter, had a daughter with Zeus and they named the child Persephone.[95] When Persephone was abducted by Hades, the god of the underworld, to be his wife, Demeter was grief-stricken. So she withheld fertility from the world, making it parched and barren. This left the people of the world with nothing to sacrifice to the gods, who in turn pressed Zeus to allow Demeter to have her child back. Zeus relented and allowed Demeter to travel to the land of Hades.

The rituals of the Mysteries then took the initiate through a descent into the underworld, a search for what one loved, and then a return to the world above with that which was cherished most. Intimately bound up in this was the concept of each person having a body but also a soul, and that their soul—their spiritual and loving side—would live forever. This seemed to have a profound effect on those who participated in the Mysteries.

Combined with this was a lavish festival celebrated each year at the time of the Greater Mysteries, which became an even more spectacular event every four years. The festival opened with sacred objects being brought from Eleusis to the Eleusinion, a temple at the foot of the Acropolis. The Eleusinion was located on the eastern side of Panathenaic Way just south of the Agora, and can still be seen today. Ritual sacrifices were made by the participants, after which the initiates washed themselves in the sea at Phaleron, about three miles south of the city. A grand procession then began at the Dipylon Gate of Athens, with large numbers of prominent individuals leading throngs of joyful people westward along the road known as the Sacred Way to the town of Eleusis.

There the initiates maintained an all-night vigil during which they fasted. Then they broke the fast with a strong drink called kykeon. Upon entering the Telesterion, a great hall able to hold thousands of people, the initiates finally received the higher Mysteries of the order. This was followed by a celebratory feast with uninhibited music and dancing. This climactic event merged new initiates with long-time members in this prestigious society.

Being part of the Eleusinian Mysteries was a powerful experience in the ancient world, and the people of Athens remained at the heart of this secret society for hundreds of years.

Unfortunately the sounds of war, which could so often be heard in the background at Athens, now became much louder. Ongoing friction between the city and its western neighbor, the city-state of Megara, resulted in the Megarian Decree being issued by Pericles in 432 BC. This edict banned all trade between Megara and any port in the Delian League—a devastating blow to that neighboring city. Megara was an ally of the Spartans at this time, and begged for their help.

That conflict came on top of the ongoing fighting at Potidaea far to the north, where Athens was battling Corinth, Sparta and their surrounding allies.[96] In 431 BC, with the Athenian siege of Potidaea still in progress, representatives of Corinth, Athens and Sparta met and—when they were unable to resolve their differences—Sparta chose to go to war. With that, the Thirty Years' Peace was broken and the devastating Second Peloponnesian War got under way.

King Archidamus II of Sparta led the opening attack in this epic war, bringing his Peloponnesian troops into Attica and starting

Fig. 49 The Eleusinian Mysteries are portrayed on this tablet found in the sanctuary at Eleusis.

Fig. 50 Pericles delivering the funeral oration

to ravage the countryside around Athens. Since the Spartans and their allies were strong enough to easily win any combat in the open field, Pericles called the people of Attica to come within the thick, protective walls of Athens where they would be safe. When those many thousands of people took refuge inside the massive walls, the enclosed city became very densely packed. Even so, the citizens survived all this turmoil because the long walls Athens had built from the city to the port of Piraeus allowed food and other supplies to arrive by sea every day.

To strike back at their attackers, the people of Athens authorized fleets of ships to plunder and sack towns along the coastline of the Peloponnese, hitting unpredictably and often. As a result both sides suffered, but without any head-to-head battles. At the end of the first year, during a lull in these hostilities, Athens performed the traditional wartime ceremony honoring its dead soldiers. We know this because Pericles delivered a remarkable funeral oration that year which was dutifully recorded by Thucydides.

This stirring oration gave a sense of why Pericles was praised for his ability to inspire and arouse his listeners. His words seemed to pick people up and carry them effortlessly in whatever direction he wanted his city to go. For this auspicious event he dispensed with the traditional eulogy and instead sought to praise those who had fallen by conjuring an image of the great city they had preserved. He told how Athens had risen to its current power and glory, its democratic and free way of life, and the honorable ways that its people conducted themselves. In part, he said:

> I shall begin by speaking about our ancestors, since it is only right and proper on such an occasion to pay them the honour of recalling what they did. In this land of ours there have always been the same people living from generation to generation up till now, and they, by their courage and their virtues, have handed it on to us, a free country. They certainly deserve our praise. Even more so do our fathers deserve it. For to the inheritance they had received they added all the empire we have now, and it was not without blood

and toil that they handed it down to us of the present generation. And then we ourselves, assembled here today, who are mostly in the prime of life, have, in most directions, added to the power of our empire and have organized our State in such a way that it is perfectly well able to look after itself both in peace and in war….

Mighty indeed are the marks and monuments of our empire which we have left. Future ages will wonder at us, as the present age wonders at us now. We do not need the praises of a Homer, or of anyone else whose words may delight us for the moment, but whose estimation of facts will fall short of what is really true. For our adventurous spirit has forced an entry into every sea and into every land; and everywhere we have left behind us everlasting memorials of good done to our friends or suffering inflicted on our enemies.

This, then, is the kind of city for which these men, who could not bear the thought of losing her, nobly fought and nobly died. [97]

Unfortunately the Spartans and their allies came back the next year to pillage the countryside of Attica. So the local people had to once again squeeze themselves within the city walls of Athens. This time, however, the congestion led to an outbreak of plague that spread quickly. It began to decimate the city's population.

Responding to this disaster, the famous physician Hippocrates was said to have come to Athens to help contain the plague. Born on the island of Kos in the Aegean Sea, about fifty miles south of Miletus, Hippocrates studied at the *asclepieion* on that island. This sacred place was dedicated to Asclepios, the god of healing, and a rustic form of medicine was practiced there. But Hippocrates took that medical profession to such a high level that he was soon called the father of medicine. A form of his Hippocratic Oath on proper professional conduct by a physician is still in use today.

Hippocrates was only thirty years of age when he came to Athens during the plague, and though stories about him were often as

Fig. 51 Hippocrates

much legend as fact, this was how his experience in the city was described.

> Observing that the only people not affected by the plague were iron smiths, Hippocrates made an astute deduction: Their resistance must somehow be related to the dry, hot atmosphere in which they worked. He promptly wrote up his prescription. The citizens of Athens were to light fires in every home to dry the atmosphere, to burn corpses, and to boil all water before consumption. The plague retreated.[98]

The hardships of war and plague weighed heavily on most of the people in Athens and someone had to bear the brunt of the blame. So it was decided to take away Pericles' title as general of the army. Yet his political leadership of the city continued. When their anger ran its course and the people of Athens realized he was still the best one to lead them in war, Pericles was soon re-elected to his military position.

But there was no appeal from the fatal nature of the disease. Pericles' two sons by his first wife perished in the plague. In compassion for his grief, and recognizing that he now had no heir, the citizens of Athens granted an exemption from their law against the children of foreigners. They voted to grant full citizenship rights to the son he had with Aspasia, including the right to inherit from him. This official act by the city was the closest thing we have to a wedding certificate between Pericles and Aspasia, because it formally recognized their long-standing relationship.

That blessing came barely in time. The plague was diminished by not yet gone, and in 429 BC it claimed the great man himself. Pericles fell victim to the plague and passed away.

ATHENS TRANSITION

Pericles had seen Athens through its darkest days and its brightest. And it was almost certainly true that none of the changes Athens went through in its many centuries of existence were as dramatic as the spectacular transition it made during Pericles' lifetime. He had stood among the broken and blackened stones of the city left behind by the Persian destruction in 479 BC—then forty years later he had walked through the almost-completed Parthenon with its gleaming white-marble floors and columns— beyond which one could see the huge, golden Athena. He saw the plays of Sophocles performed in the new Theatre of Dionysos. He built new stoas in the Agora where Socrates began to explore philosophy with his students. This had been a remarkable transformation for Athens.

Part of the credit for this incredible accomplishment goes to a weakness that previously afflicted the city. When the Persians first marched toward Athens, the few walls in existence at that time were mostly clustered around the Acropolis.[99] That meant most of the city was exposed to the vast army of approaching soldiers. So the city leaders had no choice but to evacuate the people and wealth of the city to Salamis, leaving the old buildings of Athens exposed. The Persians took the bait and leveled the city. Then they burned what was left and withdrew. What remained must have been a heart-rending sight.

But the people and wealth of the city had been saved, and that was the true beating heart of Athens. Those people flowed back into the damaged precincts and immediately began to rebuild. Much of the debris was instantly hauled away by Themistocles' immense project to build the city walls Athens desperately needed, and every broken piece of stone went into it.

Recovery projects such as raising civic buildings, restoring homes, and building ships for the Athenian navy caused full employment and attendant prosperity at all social levels in the city.

The newly-formed Delian League also sent wealth from its contributing member cities to the central treasury, which gradually came under the control of Athens. And as we saw, Pericles redirected much of these funds to increase the glories of his city and its Acropolis.

But an often-overlooked major source of the golden age of Athens was its people who survived the wars in 480 BC and 479 BC. Traditionally, the citizens of a city stayed and fought in defense of the things they owned. Had Athens done so, it seems clear that the combination of weak defenses and being vastly outnumbered would have still resulted in Persian occupation of the city. But in this case it would have been after many of the city's men were killed in the fighting, and after most of the surviving men, women and children were sold into slavery.

By evacuating the city instead, Athens preserved all its creative people, artisans, and leaders, which enabled it to rebuild the city on an even grander scale than before. These survivors included Aeschylus, Sophocles, Pericles, Phidias and many others. The survivors also included the parents of Socrates, Aristophanes and the rest of the generation which rose during the city's glory years. They all needed to survive the wars, or where would the golden age have been?

The other overriding reason for this successful transition came down to one man, and that was Pericles. This has often been noted, but usually in a vague manner referring to all his skills, led by

Fig. 52 Athenians return from Salamis rejoicing

his oratory and role as an excellent general. Yet as we see how the events of these times unfolded at Athens and all the other Greek cities, a different quality emerges.

Certainly Pericles was a great speaker and general, but Athens had many other notable speakers and generals as well. And the other Greek cities had their fair share of such men also. But what almost all those cities lacked was a sense of when to fight and when not to fight. That was one of the true arts that Pericles possessed. He was not bashful about fighting when the need arose. But he also knew when to stop fighting and sign a treaty that would give the most benefit to Athens. It was an effective weapon which he used many times. Soon we will see what happened to Athens when Pericles was no longer present to make those decisions.

The victories and treaties of Pericles created times of peace and prosperity for the people of Athens, and they used those times to produce the great works for which that age was justifiably celebrated. Pericles did not personally write any inspiring plays, carve any beautiful statues, design magnificent temples, or probe the intricate depths of philosophy. He simply created a world in which many other gifted people could do so.

That was his gift to us. A golden age.

LET LOOSE THE DOGS OF WAR

Pericles was survived by Aspasia, their son Pericles the Young-er, his youthful ward Alcibiades, and friends of the family such as Sophocles and Socrates. In fact, so many good things had been set in motion that it would be some time before the people of Athens realized what they had lost with Pericles' departure.

The historian Thucydides was in Athens at this time and, like many others, he came down with the plague. But he managed to survive. That was fortunate, because much of what we know about these times has been drawn from his highly detailed *History of the Peloponnesian War*.

Thucydides was born in Athens about 460 BC to a well-established family that owned property and gold mines in Thrace on the northern shore of the Aegean Sea. He apparently began to write about the war when it was just beginning, without knowing what a large and decisive event it was about to become.

As the heir to his family's holdings in Thrace, Thucydides had considerable influence in that area. So Athens took advantage of his connections and made him a *strategos* in 424 BC, placing him in charge of a force that occupied the island of Thasos in that region.

Fig. 53 Thucydides

When the neighboring city of Amphipolis—an ally of Athens—was attacked by Spartan troops, he rushed to help them. But by the time he arrived they had already surrendered. So Thucydides was blamed—fairly or not—by the people of Athens for that loss and exiled from the city.

As a result he took up residence on his properties in Thrace and, with the comfortable income from his gold mines, devoted his time and passion to traveling around Greece and recording the proceedings of the war. As an exile from Athens he was readily accepted into Sparta and other parts of the Peloponnese, so he could see both sides of this growing conflict. Those observations were recorded in his long *History*.

Following Pericles' death, a man named Cleon came to power in Athens. This fellow had been a prominent opponent of Pericles and was described as crude and unpolished. But he was also charismatic and gifted as an orator. In a clear change, he did not share Pericles' respect for the land power of the Spartans, and proceeded to take the fight to the enemy. These risky and aggressive moves included military sorties into the nearby states of Boeotia and Aetolia, as well as to the island of Lesbos.

But the largest expansion of this war came from the continuous raids by the Athenian fleet along the shores of the Peloponnese. This provocative activity came to a head in 425 BC when his general Demosthenes (not the latter-day orator of the same name) began to fortify an outpost on Spartan-controlled territory near the city of Pylos in the southwest corner of the Peloponnese.

Athenian occupation of this outpost was seen as a serious threat by the Spartans because the *helots* who worked like serfs on the Spartan fields—only one step better than slaves—could run away from their masters and take refuge with the Athenians at Pylos. That brought back memories of the massive *helot* revolt forty years earlier which had drained Sparta for years. So the Spartans assembled a force and attacked the Pylos outpost, hoping to drive out the Athenians.

The Spartan force took up positions on the mainland and on the island of Sphacteria which was only a short distance away from Pylos. But during the fighting, 420 Spartans became stranded on the island when additional Athenian ships arrived to join the battle. With the campaign still in doubt, Cleon decided to throw the dice and lead reinforcements from Athens to Pylos, which tipped the balance in favor of Athens. When he finally succeeded in capturing the island of Sphacteria, only 292 Spartans survived the conflict. They were taken hostage, giving Cleon a great victory.

Encouraged by this experience, Athens tried a similar ploy closer to home by setting up an outpost in enemy territory at Delium in the nearby state of Boeotia. But this time, when the Boeotian troops attacked the outpost, the supporting Athenian fleet did not arrive in time to turn the tide of battle. So the soldiers from Athens were forced to flee homeward.

One notable aspect of the Battle of Delium was that Socrates was once again acknowledged for his conduct on the battlefield, as described by Alcibiades and recorded by Plato.

> Again, gentlemen, it was worth while to see Socrates when the army was routed and retreating from Delion. I happened to be there on horseback, and he on foot. This man and Laches were retreating together in the rout…. There indeed I had an even better view of Socrates than at Poteidaia, for I had less to fear, being on horseback. First I saw how he kept his head much better than Laches; next I really thought, Aristophanes, to quote your words, that he marched exactly as he does here, "with swaggering gait and rolling eye," quietly looking round at friends and enemies, and making it quite clear to everyone even a long way off that if anyone laid a finger on this man, he would defend himself stoutly. And therefore he came off safe, both this man and his companion; for in war where men are like that, people usually don't touch them with a finger, but pursue those who are running headlong.[100]

This description suggested one reason why Socrates may have become so successful with his discussions of philosophy in Athens. His unshakeable and calm confidence allowed him—even though he began life as a stoneworker—to walk among the greatest members of the city and engage them with challenging questions, something they might not have tolerated from one who showed any sign of weakness or uncertainty.

Aspasia also went through a life change after the passing of her lover Pericles. She was left without a "man responsible for her," which was required at that time for all women in the city. Theoretically her son could have been considered "responsible" but he was only sixteen at the time. So it came about that she was married to Lysicles, an influential *strategos* and landowner. After Lysicles was killed in battle the next year, there was no record that Aspasia ever remarried. Since her son turned eighteen shortly thereafter, which gave him all the rights of a head-of-household, he reasonably became legally responsible for her support.

In any event that would have been more of a legal necessity than a monetary one. Aspasia apparently had enough financial resources with her house of courtesans or *hetaira* to support herself and stay active in social affairs. This was particularly evident in her association with Socrates, who brought associates and their wives to enjoy discussions with her.[101] The younger Alcibiades also continued his relationship with her, as witnessed by Socrates famously having to come to Aspasia's home to retrieve the fellow when he had grown up. The relationship between Aspasia, Socrates and Alcibiades was thereafter the subject of many paintings.[102]

Meanwhile, the Peloponnesian War was still raging. The Spartan general Brasidas, embarrassed by his earlier loss at Pylos, assembled a large force in 423 BC and led them all the way to Amphipolis in Thrace, about 300 miles north of Athens. This strategically important city provided Athens with large quantities of gold, silver and stout timber for making ships. When Brasidas attacked the Athenian garrison there, the battle occurred in which Thucydides arrived too late to save the city.

Thucydides did, however, take up a strong position at the seaport of Eion near Amphipolis before being relieved of his command. After a year of negotiations and armistice, Cleon came from

Athens with a fleet of thirty ships, hoping to repeat his earlier great triumph at Pylos. But the fates did not favor him this time. The battle went poorly and he died in the midst of the fighting. Among the Spartans, General Brasidas was also mortally wounded and perished shortly thereafter.

With those two hawkish leaders out of the way, the people of Athens and Sparta admitted the heavy losses they had incurred and sought a truce. So the Peace of Nicias was signed in 421 BC between these two cities and many of their allies. Two crucial parts of the treaty were that the city of Amphipolis would be returned to Athens, and the 292 Spartans captured at Sphacteria would be allowed to go home. However the promised return of Amphipolis to Athens never took place, so this treaty was broken from the start. But for now, there were a few years of peace.

The fiery early days of the Peloponnesian War had put a damper on the raising of any beautiful buildings in Athens. But after the victory at Pylos the people of Athens had begun to feel more confident about their future. So the erection of architectural wonders began to move forward again.

On the western side of the Agora, in the open space between the Bouleuterion and the Royal Stoa, there had been a small cult area devoted to Zeus. This was now replaced by a magnificent *stoa* dedicated to that same deity. It honored Zeus as the champion of freedom, as reflected in its name: the Stoa of Zeus Eleutherios.

At the time it was built, this was the largest structure in the Agora, standing an impressive 143 feet in length and 35 feet wide. Its long side faced the Agora and included a wing at each end, both of which were 35 feet wide and projected 19 feet forward toward the marketplace. A total of 25 columns were arrayed across the front of this stoa, and another nine were placed in the interior to support the roof.

Just in front of those exterior columns of the *stoa* stood a striking statue of Zeus, making it clear to all the purpose of this grand structure. And above the columns was a beautiful façade made of white Pentelic marble. Along with the Temple of Hephaistos, which stood on the low hill just behind it, this Stoa of Zeus

Fig. 54 Socrates drags Alcibiades from the house of Aspasia

brought some of the exquisite appearance of the Acropolis temples right down to the side of the Agora.

This *stoa* was also a curious structure in that it had a religious purpose but was not built like a temple. Instead it looked like a civic building suitable for informal public gatherings. And in fact Socrates was known to have met his friends and students here.

A little further to the south, the Monument of the Eponymous Heroes was built about 40 feet east of the Bouleuterion. This long pedestal was 6 feet thick and 55 feet long, with limestone used for its lower courses and polished marble for the upper part of the monument. Upon it were spaced—at equal intervals—bronze statues portraying each of the ten legendary men in whose honor the ten tribes of Athens were named. Since this wall was actually situated in the marketplace but close to the city hall it was the ideal place to post legislation, city announcements and decrees. So it became one of the favorite gathering places in the city, where one might stay abreast of all that was happening.

A few years later, in 421 BC, the citizens of Athens returned to the Acropolis with an even grander plan. Work began on a temple that would become one of the lasting landmarks of this golden age—the Erechtheion. This temple has always been instantly recognized by its porch of Caryatids, the attractive statues of women who stood in place of stone columns to support the roof.

The hallowed ground upon which it stood had been sacred since the earliest years of Athens. This site was believed to be the burial place of its first kings, as well as the location of its founding mythology. Earlier we saw that the cloistered area called the Pandroseion on the north side of the Acropolis contained the sacred olive tree that Athena was said to have given to the city. Immediately east of that tree was the well of salty water reportedly donated by Poseidon, along with the mark made when he struck the rock with his trident. Beside that were graves believed to belong to the two early kings of Athens named Cecrops and Erechtheus.

This exquisite new temple was placed directly over the kings' gravesites and the salty well—and immediately beside the olive tree. It was dedicated to the continued remembrance of those kings and deities. The entire edifice was built of gleaming white

Pentelic marble, except for the black limestone from Eleusis which decorated the frieze below the roofline.

The eastern entrance to this temple was graced by six tall columns, and behind them stood a doorway leading into its largest room. This eastern *cella* was dedicated to Athena, and it was here that the ancient wooden image of the goddess was placed. Since the Old Temple to Athena had been destroyed by the Persians, there was no better place to put the ancient relic. This relic was the embodiment of Athena, and on her was placed the beautiful *peplos* gown carried to the Acropolis in the colorful procession of the Panathenaia.

Just to the west of that richly furnished room was a slightly smaller chamber devoted to Poseidon and Erechtheus, which also contained altars for the god Hephaistos and for Voutos—the brother of Erechtheus. Below this room was a pit for Athena's sacred snake, which had been associated with the city ever since the time of Cecrops. A doorway to the north opened onto the spacious northern porch which had a roof supported by six massive columns and gave an unparalleled view over the city of Athens. Returning to the western chamber, a flight of stairs led to the elevated southern porch where the six stone Caryatids served as elegant replacements for columns around its edges. That porch and those tireless maidens looked south over the ruins of the Old Temple and toward the vast expanse of the Parthenon in all its glory.[103]

Farther west on this high plateau, the people of Athens raised another sacred building a year later. This was the Temple of Athena Nike, the goddess of victory. This small temple stood upon what was, in Mycenaean times, the site of a strategic battlement along the protective wall around the Acropolis. That battlement extended forward from this wall at a place to the right of the slope that led up to the flat top of the mountain. Archers and soldiers once stood on that platform to harass and drive away any invaders. But as the years passed and that outcropping fell into disuse, the cult of Athena Nike began to hold services there. After the surrounding Propylaia had been completed in 432 BC, this outcropping was left unfinished, with the promise of a future temple.

Fig. 55 Erechtheion Temple and the Caryatids

In 420 BC that promise was finally kept and this tiny temple to Athena Nike received its finishing touches. Due to the small platform available, the temple was only 27 feet long and just over 18 feet wide. Four columns were sufficient to support its front pediment, and four more supported a small porch at the back. Made completely of the traditional shining-white Pentelic marble, its entrance faced east toward the Propylaia. Entering the temple from that direction, one saw its main attraction, a famous statue of Athena Nike. This representation of the goddess—unlike the usual portrayal of winged victory—showed her without wings. That led to this statue being called *apteros Nike*. And it was said that she was not given wings so victory would never leave the city.

Unfortunately there could not be victory without war, and more acts of war soon became visible on the horizon.

ALCIBIADES,
THUNDER AND LIGHTNING

While the citizens of Athens made the most of their fragile truce by enriching the city, the people of the Peloponnesus found themselves torn asunder by civil war. The states of Argolis, Elis and parts of Arcadia had been chafing under the overlordship of Sparta for many years. So after the Spartan loss at Pylos—along with the especially humiliating surrender of its troops there—they were quick to focus on these signs of weakness. Thus encouraged, the three states formed an alliance of defiance.

This act was applauded in Athens, especially by Alcibiades who was now thirty-two years of age and starting to follow in the footsteps of his honored relative and guardian, Pericles. Yet he pursued this task from a completely different direction. It was Alcibiades' good fortune to be born handsome, rich, and under the wing of the greatest man in Athens. Unfortunately that attracted flatterers like vultures hungry for food, and turned his head.

However, it was rather his love of distinction and love of fame to which his corrupters appealed, and thereby plunged him all too soon into ways of presumptuous scheming, persuading him that he had only to enter public life, and he would straightway cast into total eclipse the ordinary generals and public leaders, and not only that, he would even surpass Pericles in power and reputation among the Hellenes....

But the love of Socrates, though it had many powerful rivals, somehow mastered Alcibiades. For he was of good natural parts, and the words of his teacher took hold of him and wrung his heart and brought tears to his eyes. But sometimes he would surrender himself to the flatterers who tempted him with many pleasures, and slip away from Socrates, and suffer himself to be actually hunted down by him like a runaway slave. And yet he feared and reverenced Socrates alone, and despised the rest of his lovers.

Plutarch
Alcibiades 6:1-3

Given his distinguished heritage, Alcibiades became an astute general. He was also an accomplished orator, and a surprisingly effective back-room dealer in political affairs. But unlike Pericles, the younger man favored direct war with Sparta—a difficult path. And as a result Alcibiades became an avid supporter of the rebelling Peloponnesian states.

Since those three states together ruled a continuous strip of land across the middle of the Peloponnesus, from the east coast to the west coast, their rebellion cut off Sparta from its northern allies at Corinth and Thebes. The only visible weakness of the allies was that not all of Arcadia had joined their alliance. In fact the key city of Tegea committed itself to Sparta. So in 418 BC the rebellious allies, led by the city of Argos and its Argive troops, assembled a large force and marched southward toward Tegea. Alcibiades persuaded his fellow Athenians to entrust him with 1000 soldiers and marched out to join the rebels.

The Spartans quickly realized that the loss of Tegea would leave them isolated in the southern Peloponnesus and reduce

Fig. 56 Alcibiades

them to an insignificant power in Greece. So they rapidly assembled a similar force and marched north of Tegea to intercept the Argive armies. The clash of these two waves of soldiers near the city of Mantinea became the largest land battle in the entire Peloponnesian War. Although the allies did well at first, the Spartans eventually won the day. By so doing they re-established their reputation as a major land power. And by forcing the rebels to break up their alliance Sparta moved once more to the head of the states in the Peloponnesus.

So Sparta won a great moral victory. But the heavy fighting had weakened all the states in this large peninsula. And Athens still held a position of commanding strength. So all was well for the city beside the Acropolis—until disaster struck in Sicily.

A cultural divide existed on Sicily, just as it did in much of Greece, between those who considered themselves to be Ionian in culture as opposed to those who were Doric. There were only small differences in language and culture between the two camps, but it seemed quite real to the people involved. This became a growing source of friction because Athens and most of the members of its empire across the Aegean Sea saw themselves as Ionian. Meanwhile Sparta and many of its allies touted their Doric heritage. And those same political tensions extended to the island of Sicily as well.

Many towns in Sicily had been founded by Ionian Greek cities and still maintained strong alliances with them. Athens used this to its advantage and set up solid trade relations and political ties with these Sicilian towns.

On the other hand, Syracuse—the largest city on Sicily—was of Doric descent and naturally aligned itself with Sparta. So there was already some cultural friction and suspicion between the two groups. This became inflamed by fears among leaders in the small towns that Syracuse was planning to use its size to dominate them and take away their independence.

Those fears turned out to be justified. When Syracuse interfered in the politics of its smaller neighbor Leontini, an appeal was sent to Athens for help. For whatever reason, no help was given. But when that was followed by another appeal from the town of Segesta in 415 BC, Athens realized this was a large issue and perhaps a great opportunity. By joining the small towns against Syracuse they could not only remove the growing Spartan influence on this richly productive island but also change Sicily into a greater contributor to Athenian trade and prosperity. But this feeling was not unanimous.

Alcibiades stood strongly in favor of sending the fleet and reaping these enticing benefits. But General Nicias and his supporters were opposed to launching any relief expedition to Sicily. So the issue was hotly debated—but eventually the voters sided with Alcibiades to send the fleet. To mollify all parties, three generals were named to lead the expedition: Alcibiades, Nicias and an older general named Lamachus.

But the opponents of Alcibiades were not yet done. When someone destroyed a number of stone markers dedicated to the god Hermes which were placed around Athens for good luck, Alcibiades was accused of the crime. He vehemently denied it, and demanded an instant trial to clear his name before the expedition sailed. His opponents, however, wisely refused to press charges until after the fleet had left the harbor. They realized Alcibiades was enormously popular in the military. By waiting until many of his supporters had sailed with him, Alcibiades' opponents then held a clear majority in any voting and jury in the city. The charges against him were easily endorsed.

Meanwhile, the three generals on the flagship of the fleet continued to argue on their way to Sicily. They were sharply divided about how to fight the coming campaign. Nicias proposed an extremely limited effort. Since the immediate cause of the current expedition was to assist Segesta in its fight with the town of Selinus, a Syracuse ally, he proposed doing only that much, then returning home.

Alcibiades argued in favor of obtaining allies from as many cities on Sicily as possible in a short amount of time, then launching a massive attack on Syracuse. He knew the people of Athens wanted some payback for the cost of the expedition and he proposed to give it to them.

General Lamachus was just a simple soldier at heart. Instead of wasting time gathering allies, he advocated sailing directly into

Fig. 57 Cities in Sicily and Magna Graecia

Syracuse harbor with the large fleet of 134 ships they had amassed, and beating the city into submission.

After much heated discussion, the three men agreed to go with the plan put forth by Alcibiades. But just as they arrived at Sicily with their large fleet a messenger appeared with word that Alcibiades had been brought up on charges—and was required to return to Athens immediately to stand trial. Outraged, Alcibiades boarded a ship and headed home. The campaign in Sicily spiraled downward from there.

The Athenian force landed at the harbor of Catania about thirty miles north of Syracuse. With the recruiting of local allies going slowly, they grew impatient and launched an attack against Syracuse anyway. The Athenian troops were successful in this first encounter outside the city. But they were stalemated when the Syracuse soldiers retreated inside the city walls, so the Athenians were forced to pull back to Catania for the winter.

Meanwhile Alcibiades was busy as well. When the ship returning him to Athens docked at a port on the Italian mainland, he escaped from his bailiffs. He was under no illusions about what would happen upon his arrival at Athens, where his supporters were now heavily outnumbered. So instead of waiting for a guilty verdict and sentencing, he made his way to Sparta.

Just as he feared, word of his conviction and the sentence of death arrived shortly thereafter. That outraged Alcibiades even further. At the same time it made him quite popular in Sparta, even if he was still treated with a measure of suspicion. Having been decisively cast out at home, he could see no other way forward than to make his bed with the Spartans. So he slowly began giving them advice about the plans of Athens. He urged them to send a Spartan general and reinforcements to Syracuse, which they did. That helped to turn the tide of war in favor of Syracuse and Sparta.

When the Spartan general Gylippus arrived in Syracuse, he organized the defense of the city while continuing to fight the many skirmishes caused by both sides jockeying for position. During one of those small battles the Athenian general Lamachus was killed, leaving Nicias alone at the head of a force being whittled down by the fighting. When he appealed to Athens for help, two more generals were sent at the head of 73 ships and more than 5000 soldiers. This was the equivalent of going all-in during a poker game and betting everything you have. The stakes in this war had gotten exceedingly high.

When the reinforcements arrived, pitched battles were already under way on land and sea. Yet despite this additional force, the Athenians were unable to make headway. Terrible casualties were suffered on both sides, leading the Athenian generals to believe there was no way to prevail. So they agreed amongst themselves to withdraw to Athens. But before they could act, a lunar eclipse cast an ominous sign. So the departure was delayed. And the delay proved fatal.

Syracuse used this time to blockade the entrance to the harbor, trapping the Athenian ships inside where they had little room to maneuver. A major part of the Athenian force perished in the ensuing naval battle. The remaining Athenian troops retreated to the shore and tried to flee inland. But the forces from Syracuse and Sparta came in hot pursuit and unmercifully killed the Athenian soldiers or pressed them into slavery.

This was a devastating blow to Athens. In a single campaign the greater part of all the Athenian ships were destroyed. And the staggering casualties had slaughtered the cream of her fighting men.[104] Athens was left so weak that it could not even defend its own territory. And Sparta was poised to strike again.

Still stuck among the Spartans and facing the death penalty in Athens, Alcibiades could see no alternative to aiding the leaders of Sparta, come what may. So he suggested the Spartan generals proceed into the heart of Attica where they could occupy and fortify the small town of Decelea north of Athens. They took his advice and—once situated there—the Spartan force showed it could not be removed.

This cut off the land route for food coming into Athens, leaving the city wholly dependent on supplies bought in by sea. It also gave the Spartans a base for raiding the countryside. That in turn forced the Athenians to withdraw from the outlying areas and find shelter within the city walls, just as they had done in the last years of Pericles.

Meanwhile the members of the Delian League saw how much Athens' defeat in Sicily had weakened it at home, and that was enough to encourage some of them to go into open revolt. Alcibiades used this fact to improve his position in Sparta during 412 BC by persuading the leaders of that city to entrust him with a small fleet of ships to help those cities break free of Athens. They approved his plan so he set sail at the head of a strong force.

But while he was on this mission around the Aegean Sea he learned some disturbing news. King Agis of Sparta had ordered the admiral of the Spartan fleet to kill Alcibiades.

Actually, he should not have been too surprised by this, for the cause of the king's ire was well known.

> While Agis the king was away on his campaigns, Alcibiades corrupted Timaea his wife, so that she was with child by him and made no denial of it. When she had given birth to a male child, it was called Leotychides in public, but in private the name which the boy's mother whispered to her friends and attendants was Alcibiades. Such was the passion that possessed the woman. But he, in his mocking way, said he had not done this thing for a wanton insult, nor at the behest of mere pleasure, but in order that descendants of his might be kings of the Lacedaemonians. Such being the state of things, there were many to tell the tale to Agis, and he believed it.
>
> Plutarch
> *Alcibiades 23:7-8*

Having worn out his welcome among the Spartans, Alcibiades was forced to make another transition in his life. He fled to the southwestern part of Anatolia where an influential Persian satrap ruled the local people.[105] This was a daring step because Athens had always been regarded by the Persians as their main opponent among the Greeks. Their enmity was kept alive by the fact that almost all the Greek towns along the Aegean coast of Anatolia were ruled by Athens, and her fleets kept the Persians from making any advances there.

Sparta on the other hand was preoccupied with gaining dominance over all the Greek cities on the mainland and expressed no further ambition against Persia. Seeing the Spartans were no threat, and were the enemy of Athens, the Persian satrap had long ago decided to exploit this situation. So he was secretly funneling money to Sparta to aid it in crushing their common enemy.

Now that Alcibiades had arrived in Persian lands, with death warrants following him from Athens and Sparta, the satrap decided to take advantage of that and use this man-without-a-home as an advisor on Greek affairs. Alcibiades accepted the position, but quickly began pursuing an agenda of his own.

What he really wanted was to have the city of Athens cancel his death sentence and restore his prestigious status as general. To make a long story short, he was willing to go through another transformation if they would have him.

To implement this plan he made a risky decision and quietly attempted to win over the Athenian fleet that was now based at the island of Samos, not far from Persian territory. This was a dangerous move because the fleet was there to put down the revolts that he had helped to stir up while assisting Sparta.

Yet in spite of all that had happened, the members of the Athenian navy still held Alcibiades in high regard and listened to his appeal. The generals liked his idea of changing the leadership in Athens in a way that would help the city out of its worsening fortunes. But they were completely split on the proposal to restore his position as a general.

The surprising outcome of all this was that two of the existing generals at Samos set sail for Athens in 411 BC to argue for a new government. There they persuaded the majority of citizens to go along with setting up a narrow oligarchy called "The Four Hundred." It replaced the venerable democracy that had been established and nurtured by Solon, Cleisthenes and Pericles. It was a shocking development.

When word of this reached the fleet in Samos there was widespread disbelief. The thousands of Athenian soldiers and rowers were outraged that the generals and some powerful aristocrats had overthrown their government. So they pledged to stand by their democracy and promptly threw out the remaining senior officers, electing new generals in their place.

For one of the new generals they chose an exceptionally capable junior officer named Thrasybulus who had just turned thirty. This young officer would be critical to the future of Athens. He was from a well-established family in that city and had grown up admiring Alcibiades, who was nine years older. One of the first things Thrasybulus did in his position as general was to offer safe passage to Alcibiades if he would come talk with the troops at Samos—and possibly win his desired reinstatement that way. Alcibiades came, the men were electrified by his oratory and promises, and they elected him to be a general alongside Thrasybulus.

This gave Alcibiades a substantial part of what he was seeking. But it did not remove the death sentence against him nor allow him to return to Athens. When many soldiers in the fleet called for an attack on Athens to fight back against the usurpers, he calmed them and told them civil war was not the answer. Not only was civil war a bad idea under any circumstances, but it also would not win him friends among the people of that city, which was something he desperately needed at this juncture.

His patience paid off. The Spartans won a naval victory at Euboea, just north of Attica, which caused that whole state to switch its allegiance to Sparta. This caused panic in Athens. With such a disastrous loss at their doorstep, the Athenians deposed "The Four Hundred" and installed a wider oligarchy known as "The Five Thousand." This new regime promptly invited Alcibiades to return to the city. But no mention was made of the death warrant against him so he stayed away. His only hope was to give good service to Athens in his role as a general of the fleet and see what happened.

His opportunity came in the spring of the following year. The small fleet under his command joined with the Athenian fleets led by Thrasybulus and two other generals. Together they defeated a combined Spartan and Persian force at the Hellespont near Byzantium.[106] The Spartans, with their fleet destroyed, offered to make peace, but the celebrating people of Athens rejected that offer.[107]

It was decisions such as this one that showed how much the leadership of Pericles was sorely missed. With the Spartan fleet smashed, Athens had *carte-blanche* to write a treaty giving itself concessions and peace. With that, their golden age could continue as strongly as before. Instead the sane approach was rejected, and the bitter results of the Peloponnesian War were brought a step closer.

In one positive development, democracy was restored to Athens a few months later. But for Alcibiades it was not enough. Even with that change and a successful campaign, he still did not feel certain of a safe return to Athens. So he stayed at the head of his fleet and continued to fight her opponents in the northern Aegean.

After moving from victory to victory he finally returned in 407 BC to the city of his birth. All of Athens received him with a hero's welcome. The charges against him were formally dropped, and he was named commander of all the city's land and sea forces. It had been a long odyssey, but he had completed his transition back to his former life. He was home again and there was great hope in Athens.

Yet his days of basking in the bright lights of glory proved to be fleeting. A year later, Alcibiades set out with 100 ships to fight the new Spartan fleet at Ephesus on the eastern shore of the Aegean Sea. Unable to draw the Spartans into battle, he decided to leave his inactive fleet at anchor and take 20 ships to help his friend Thrasybulus who was besieging the city of Phocaea about 60 miles away.

While Alcibiades was gone, the man he left in charge of the remaining fleet disobeyed direct orders and attacked the Spartans. That blunder caused a disaster in which many of the 80 ships were lost. But as the commander, Alcibiades was assessed the blame for this costly rout. Not waiting for a new trial or condemnation from Athens, Alcibiades retired to the northern end of the Aegean Sea and played no further significant role in the war. That was the final turn in a career that had been filled with many reverses.

It was said that Alcibiades came into considerable wealth in Anatolia, and passed the rest of his days in the company of courtesans. He left the people of Athens in the company of war.

Fig. 58 Alcibiades and his courtesans,
a painting by Félix Auvray (1800-1833)

SOCRATES, PLATO
AND ARISTOTLE

Thrasybulus was punished for his role in the naval defeat by having his position of *strategos* stripped away. Yet in a strange twist of fate, losing that honor saved his life—and had serious repercussions for the city of Athens.

That unusual course of events began a few months later in 406 BC, when Thrasybulus was commander of a single trireme ship in the Battle of Arginusae just east of the island of Lesbos. This became a great Athenian victory, but only after many ships were destroyed on both sides. The generals in charge of this engagement left Thrasybulus and the commander of another ship to stay and rescue the Athenian sailors who were floating among the debris of the lost ships. Then those generals led the rest of the fleet in pursuit of the fleeing Spartan vessels. Unfortunately a sudden storm drove the two rescue ships to shore, and by the time they could put to sea again, all the sailors were dead. Somewhere between 1000 and 5000 men died, depending on who told the story.

The grieving families in Athens demanded blood, and the generals were offered up. Since he was not a general, no charges were filed against Thrasybulus and his life was spared. The accused generals were promptly found guilty and executed.

One of those generals who perished was a young man full of promise who never had a chance to demonstrate what he could do. His name was Pericles the Younger. This was a terrible shock to his mother, Aspasia. First she had lost Pericles, the boy's father, to the plague—and now she lost her son. It was generally believed that Aspasia passed away herself within a few years of this tragic twist of fate.[108]

In 405 BC the Spartans won another victory at the Battle of Aegospotami in the Hellespont waterway that led to Byzantium and the Black Sea. This was a singular defeat in which almost the entire remaining Athenian fleet was destroyed.

That loss of sea power allowed the Spartans to blockade the port of Piraeus and cut off the supply of food that had been coming to Athens by sea. Suffering from starvation, the citizens of Athens conceded defeat in 404 BC. With that, the epic Peloponnesian War came to an end. Athens had its long-walls-to-the-sea torn down, its last ships were destroyed, and its overseas possessions were stripped away.

The city's golden age was grievously wounded.

Thus began the rule of the Thirty Tyrants. Sparta turned control of Athens over to thirty local aristocrats with the understanding that they would dismantle the democratic institutions and dispel the anti-Spartan sentiment in the city. The Thirty immediately set about their mission with a will. Led by Critias, who was an associate of Socrates but clearly not a philosopher, the Thirty killed at least 1500 leading citizens of Athens. They were zealous in rooting out democracy and suppressing any opposition to their rule.[109] Many people were exiled and their property confiscated in a concerted effort to enrich the Thirty and their supporters.

Yet the more aggressively these men pursued their draconian measures, the stronger the resistance became. One of the first people expelled by the Thirty was former general Thrasybulus, who was still a strong supporter of democracy. That proved to be a fatal mistake on their part. Within a year he assembled 1000 men from the countryside and stormed into Piraeus, seizing the for-

Fig. 59 Thrasybulus receiving an olive crown in Athens

tress on Munychia Hill. When the Thirty tried to force him out of
that position with the help of the local Spartan garrison, the tyrants were routed and their leader Critias was killed. The surviving members of the Thirty fled to Eleusis.

After some negotiations, Thrasybulus made a victorious entrance into Athens where he was given an olive crown by the rejoicing citizens. With his guidance, a new democratic government
was established in this city, under the watchful eye of Athena,
where that tradition had long flourished.

While those tumultuous contests were taking place—war
against peace and oligarchy against democracy—somehow life
went on in this charmed city. The resourceful people of Athens
continued to create, build and live as best they could.

To reaffirm the importance of their democratic government, a
new Bouleuterion was built directly to the west of the old one.
Slightly more compact in size at 53 feet by 72 feet, it still provided
seating for over 500 people on 12 rows of semi-circular benches.
These may have been designed with the benches placed at slightly
higher levels as one moved to the rear, which would have given
much better acoustics and visibility than the old design. The regal
entrance on the south side was marked by four tall columns, with
an impressive porch being added at a later date.

The old Bouleuterion was kept in service as a repository for all
the official records of the city. Since the mother of all the Olympian gods, Rhea, was considered the guardian of these laws, a gold-
and-ivory statue of her was placed in this building, and a small
cult area was devoted to her there. That led to the new name for
this building, the Metroon.

Another impressive addition to the Agora at this time was the
massive South Stoa. It stretched an amazing 264 feet, covering the
whole distance from the Aiakeion to the Southeast Fountainhouse.
The long north side stood open to the marketplace and was supported by more than twenty columns. Fifteen feet inside the stoa
stood a second row of columns that supported the roof,[110] then
fifteen feet farther into it was a long wall running the full length of
the building. This wall was pierced by fifteen doorways, each

leading to a roughly square room sixteen feet deep.[111] These rooms were believed to have been dining rooms where city officials ate at public expense. The large open space in front of those rooms—lined by the two rows of columns—would have been available for public use.

On the other side of the fountainhouse a new Mint was built to make the bronze coins of Athens, while the silver coinage was still struck elsewhere. This was necessary because the coinage of Athens had essentially become the standard for the entire Aegean region. This square building was about 92 feet on a side, with its northern half being a protected courtyard for the security of the coin-making operations. Furnaces used for melting the metal and pouring these coins were located in a large room at the southwest corner of the mint. Two smaller rooms built beside it were used for striking the coins with their distinctive designs, then storing them until they could be put into distribution.

Spending those shiny new coins were the crowds of men and women in Athens. As people will do, they continued to marry and have children during those tumultuous days. Their children then grew up, taking the place of elderly Athenians, and became the new aristocratic landowners, pottery-makers, playwrights and soldiers. They voted for new representatives, laws, generals and *ostracism*. And they created beautiful new buildings, statues and philosophical understandings.

Yet even among all these gifted people, one man consistently raised his contributions to legendary status—and that was Socrates. We saw his modest origin as a stonemason and subsequent rise to the full-time practice of philosophy. In this distinguished role he conversed with the richest and most influential people in this dynamic society.

He also was well-known for educating the children of these notable personages in Athens. A man named Chaerephon served as his long-time assistant and was said to have arranged the classes and tutorials that Socrates taught.

Oddly enough, Socrates made a point of loudly claiming he was not a paid instructor. That may have had something to do with his desire to fit in with the powerful people whose company

Fig. 60 Xenophon

he kept. Those individuals lived on the rich proceeds of estates they owned in the countryside, and by-and-large they did not stoop to do paid work. Over time, Socrates developed a reputation for sitting with these individuals as an equal, rather than as a paid worker. And he scrupulously kept up that image.

Step by step he rose above the other philosophers of his age such as Anaxagoras and Zeno. This came about not only through the volume and quality of his dialogues and teachings, but also through the excellence and dedication of his students. These included Plato, Xenophon and others who preserved his lessons and logic so that they came down to us through the centuries.

Xenophon was born around 430 BC in a suburb of Athens to a family wealthy enough to place him with Socrates for an education.[112] He famously came back to seek Socrates' advice in 401 BC when Cyrus, the younger brother of the Persian king, was recruiting Greeks to fight in his campaign to seize the Persian crown. Xenophon decided to go on that expedition and it was surprisingly successful—right up to the point where Cyrus was killed in a battle near Babylon.

Having lost the man who hired them, the 10,000 Greek soldiers were left stranded behind enemy lines. So they chose Xenophon as one of the men to lead them in their desperate fight to escape Persian territory and return home. He wrote an extensive account of this campaign into and out of Persia which was titled *Anabasis* and it became his greatest work.

Xenophon's other major historical work was the comprehensive *Hellenica*. This detailed account of Greek history picked up where Thucydides' *History of the Peloponnesian War* ended. It then described the people and epic events that rose to public view from 411 to 362 BC. Xenophon also treasured his days as a student of Socrates, and wrote several dialogues about him.[113]

Then, of course, there was Socrates' most famous student Plato. As almost every school-child knows, Plato was our greatest source of knowledge about Socrates and his teachings. This young man came from a rich, well-established family, and some of his relatives were already associates of Socrates. So when Plato's father died, the young man had enough funds to do as he wished and

Fig. 61 Plato

attached himself to the philosopher. Since he only turned eighteen in 409 BC,[114] Plato was not present at many of Socrates' dialogues. His extensive knowledge of those fascinating discussions must have come from the lessons taught to him by Socrates or from testimony by his relatives and others who were present at those events.

These dialogues explored many aspects of Greek society and gave a candid look into those days. They also stirred so many intriguing thoughts about life, religion, government and morality that they have been studied and taught down to the present day.

Perhaps the most celebrated of these dialogues was *The Republic*, where Socrates discussed justice, the just man and the just city-state. In the course of doing that he explored with several Athenians and foreigners the different types of people who gave rise to different kinds of states: timocracy,[115] oligarchy,[116] democracy and tyranny.[117] As we have seen, the people of Athens had experience with each of these over the years. He concluded that the best ruler would be a philosopher-king, and then talked about how people could be educated and trained to become that kind of leader. Although their conclusions were their own, these wide-ranging discussions have proved to be stimulating and relevant to many people over the centuries.

Two other dialogues, *The Apology* and *Phaedo*, conveyed the trial of Socrates, his last days, and his last thoughts. As suggested in these dialogues and other historical records, the charges against him for corrupting the young and not believing in the gods of the state were simply a convenient excuse to convict and exile him. The reason for this animosity against him has often been explained as "he was a gadfly" who bothered powerful men. And that was almost certainly true to some degree. But he had been doing this for decades and never been brought to trial in that time. Did something happen in more recent years? As it turned out, there seemed to have been a widespread perception in Athens that Socrates was too close to Critias, the head of the Thirty Tyrants who caused so much bloodshed and suffering in the city.

This may well have been due to Socrates' close relationship with Critias many years earlier, before the man became the dominant ruler of Athens. In those days Critias was a writer of plays and poems of serious reflection. So there was good reason for the two men to know each other and develop a mutual respect. What happened after that was the part which became muddled.

During his trial Socrates tried to put some distance between himself and Critias by telling a story in which he had refused to cooperate with the Thirty when they ordered him to bring in a popular advocate for democracy so that the man could be executed. But that was a two-edged sword. If Socrates gave such a refusal, people would have expected him to be executed at that moment, as the tyrants had done with others. The fact that Socrates went unpunished may have been seen as a sign of favoritism towards him, strengthening the claims of his link to the Thirty.

In any event, the tyrants had fallen and been driven from the city. The advocates of democracy—whose families had suffered deprivations and deaths among their family members—were in power again and showed a strong desire to punish those associated with the tyrants' regime. Some angry people wanted Socrates eliminated, and the court supported them.

Even so, it was not clear that anyone wanted Socrates to die as a result of his trial. It was traditional in those days for the accused to propose an alternate sentence, such as exile. This allowed the court to show leniency by agreeing to the exile, thereby extending an olive branch to the supporters of the person who was being sent away. Socrates clearly shocked all parties involved by not only failing to suggest exile but even proposing that he be rewarded with free meals for the rest of his life as his "sentence."

He had a second chance to avoid the death penalty when his friends arranged for him to escape from jail and flee the country. But again he refused. Some suggested that he did not want to put his friends at risk of retribution in this way, and that may indeed have played a part in his thoughts. Yet it is also worthy of notice that his many teachings clearly show Athens was his city and his life. He had been one of the jewels illuminating its society, and most of the people he loved had lived and died there. His words to his friends seemed to carry the feeling that he could not bear to start again in some other place. So he stayed, wished the best for his city and those who loved him, and drank the hemlock that

Fig. 62 Socrates drinks the fatal hemlock

ended his life. And with that, one of the bright lights that had lit the golden age of Athens went out.

After his mentor was no longer there to guide him, Plato took some time in private to write his first eleven dialogues, beginning with *The Apology*.[118] In these dialogues Socrates spoke with people from different walks of life and asked questions that elicited new insights. It is worthy of note that no writings by Socrates have ever been found. As a result, these dialogues recorded by Plato have proved to be our best source of all his teachings.

During this time Plato was believed to have also traveled to Sicily and Egypt. He then returned to Athens in 387 BC, and created his school known as the Academy shortly thereafter. The school was located in a grove of olive trees two-thirds of a mile northwest of Athens, just outside the Dipylon Gate area. This Academy has been credited as the first school of higher education in the Western World.

There was no question that these were unsettling times for Athens and the other Greek cities. Athens' fall had left Sparta as the dominant power in Greece, and the Spartans' heavy-handed manner did not sit well with many of the other cities. So Corinth, Thebes, Athens and Argos combined to fight Sparta on land and on the sea.[119] This war ended inconclusively in 387 BC, but even so Athens benefitted.

That happened because the fighting kept Sparta away long enough for Athens to rebuild its long walls from the city to its port at Piraeus. This vastly improved its defensive strength and assured the city of a food supply in case of another siege. The Athenian navy was slowly built up as well, and a number of islands that had been part of its "empire" before were now brought under its control again. In other words, some of the damage wrought by the Peloponnesian War was being reversed and Athens was recovering a portion of her strength.

The other winner in this fighting was Persia. It had thrown its support to Sparta late in the war due to strong fears over the growing Athenian influence in the Aegean region. In return, Sparta wrote into the resulting peace agreement that Persia would receive control over all the Greek cities on the eastern coast of the Aegean from Phocaea to Miletus. That move put those cities out of reach for the recovering city of Athens.

Yet these were war-torn times, and a more decisive battle was not long in coming. Thebes revolted against Sparta again in 371 BC, and the result was a major battle at Leuctra, seven miles southwest of Thebes. The utter defeat of the Spartans and the death of their king seriously damaged Sparta's confidence and the credibility of their claim to lead the cities of Greece.

Meanwhile, at the Academy in Athens, Plato not only continued to teach his students but also wrote what are usually called his "middle" dialogues.[120] These included the celebrated *Republic* as well as his popular *Symposium* which explored the nature of love.

Around 367 BC he traveled to Syracuse in Sicily, where he was a guest at the city's magnificent court. But while there, he got on the wrong side of the tyrant of that city and was sentenced to death. When his sentence was commuted to being sold into slavery, he was purchased by a friend who set him free.

Apparently Plato taught better than he learned, because a few years later—after the tyrant had died—he was back in Syracuse tutoring the man's son. Caught up once again in the political turmoil there, Plato was held against his will until he eventually managed to get free and returned to Athens. Suffice it to say he then retreated into academic life and applied himself to writing. This produced his collection of "later" dialogues.[121]

While teaching at the Academy, Plato had many students who went on to play significant roles in society, but none more so than Aristotle. Born in 384 BC in the region of Chalcidice on the northern coast of the Aegean Sea, Aristotle was fortunate to have a father who was the personal physician to the king of Macedonia. So he grew up with a significant amount of education, and at the age of eighteen was sent to Athens to study under Plato at the Academy. He stayed for nineteen years, during which time he was said to have assisted in the education of the younger students there.

Fig. 63 Aristotle

Some of the close friends Aristotle made at the Academy were destined to achieve a measure of glory in their own right. One of those was Xenocrates, who was a little older and had accompanied their mentor Plato to Syracuse in 361 BC. Another young man named Hermias joined Aristotle at the Academy after having been a slave to the ruler of Atarneus, a city on the eastern shore of the Aegean facing the island of Lesbos. Hermias had managed to win his freedom and greatly impressed the ruler, who apparently paid for his former slave to attend the Academy. When his rich sponsor died, Hermias returned to Atarneus as the man's heir and became the ruler of that land.

In 347 BC their incomparable teacher Plato passed away. Faced with that loss, Aristotle felt he had stayed long enough and went with Xenocrates to call on their friend Hermias. A young student named Theophrastos accompanied them, serving as Aristotle's assistant. Hermias welcomed them and offered to support Aristotle and Theophrastos in the work they wanted to do on the nearby island of Lesbos. With that encouragement, the two men launched into a serious study of botany and zoology there. Aristotle apparently was studying Hermias' daughter Pythias as well, because they became married shortly thereafter.

In a surprising turn of events the king of Macedonia—Philip II —summoned Aristotle in 343 BC to teach his teenage son Alexander. It was a great honor, but Aristotle put it all at risk by naming a high price. His home town of Stageira in Chalcidice had been captured and leveled by Philip, and all its people were sold into slavery. Aristotle said he would come if Philip would re-build the town, buy back the people, and set them free to live there again. Philip agreed, and all those things were done. So Aristotle kept his word and came to Macedonia to teach Alexander.

It was a remarkable time to be in Macedonia because that land in Northern Greece was in the middle of a steep ascent from obscurity to glory. Philip II had an excellent military mind and with great determination had taken this sleepy, backwater kingdom and made it a growing power.

The leading cities of Greece had helped him with this by fighting a costly battle in 362 BC at Mantinea in the Peloponnesus.

Fig. 64 King Phillip II of Macedon
father of Alexander the Great

At that time Thebes was the major challenger to Sparta by virtue of its hard-earned victory over the Spartans nine years earlier. In this withering rematch Thebes won the battle, but its top leaders all died in the fighting. Sparta suffered a crushing defeat, and would never again be a significant power in Greece. Thebes had theoretically won, but it was rudderless and adrift.

That opened the way for Philip, who had become king of Macedonia three years later upon the deaths of his older brothers. He immediately set out to strengthen his kingdom. Forced to defend his small country from its neighbors, he then turned the tables on them and set out on a shrewd series of expansionary campaigns. One city at a time he worked his way eastward across Thrace and then south into the Greek heartland.

Aristotle came to Macedonia while all these wars were raging, which meant Philip was often absent on his campaigns. So the educator established a small school at Mieza, forty miles west of Thessaloniki, to educate his thirteen-year-old charge, Alexander.

Many heads of noble Macedonian families immediately submitted their own sons to be educated alongside Alexander, knowing that he would be their future king. These young men included Ptolemy, Hephaestion and Cassander who would play important roles in Alexander's life. Some of these students became the elite unit known as Companions, the trusted circle of officers around the young conqueror on his campaigns.

Alexander's classroom education was interrupted from time to time when his father took him on military actions—which could be looked upon as education in the field. Philip and his son left on a major campaign in 338 BC that resulted in the epic Battle of Chaeronea. Using the excuse of coming to the aid of Delphi in its dispute with a neighbor, Philip brought his army all the way down to that city in central Greece. Since Athens was in a state of war with Macedonia, the people who lived around the Acropolis had no doubt as to Philip's real intentions. So a hasty alliance was formed with Thebes and other Greek city-states to oppose Philip and drive him out. The opposing armed camps then met at Chaeronea just east of Delphi.

Philip commanded the main force of Macedonians on the right flank, but entrusted all of the left to Alexander. In so doing he took the precaution of surrounding his son with young companions and experienced officers. But if the father was cautious, the son was not. Alexander led his companions diagonally across the center of the field and split the allies' army in half, forcing it to begin a retreat. Philip's force completed the rout. When the dust had cleared, Philip was visibly in command of all of Greece. He could have gone on to besiege and destroy the leading Greek cities if he so wished, since they did not have enough strength left to oppose him. But he offered lenient terms instead, thereby recruiting them as allies for the great campaign he had in mind.[122]

This campaign was a massive invasion of Persia, which had been Philip's dream for a long time. Xenophon's *Anabasis* clearly documented the earlier campaign of 10,000 Greeks who successfully marched deep into the Persian lands. That detailed account showed step-by-step how to win such a campaign. Philip was so fascinated by this prospect that he announced to all the Greek cities his intention to lead them on this glorious endeavor.

As the preparations for that campaign were going forward, however, tragedy struck. Philip was attending his daughter's wedding when he was killed by one of his own bodyguards. The fallen king's sword was raised by Alexander, who was immediately proclaimed king of Macedonia and commander of all the Greek lands. Showing no hesitation—just like his father— Alexander stepped into that demanding role. He asserted his authority strongly over all his lands and allies, and continued preparations for the coming campaign into Persia.

Whatever Aristotle had done to help train such a confident and capable young man must have been a great source of pride to the graying teacher. But clearly the day-to-day needs of running a kingdom and conquering a world left Alexander little time for the classroom. So with the young king's warm thanks, Aristotle left Macedonia and returned to Athens.

He found the city had been well-treated by the Macedonians, even after Athens lost the most recent war. Clearly the upcoming campaign into Persia required support from a good navy, and

Macedonia had few ships of its own. So Athens was encouraged to prosper and build more vessels. And prosper it did. The full height of the golden age did not return, but even so it was a good time to be in Athens.

His close friend Xenocrates was now the headmaster or *scholarch* at the Academy, and it would have been comfortable for Aristotle to return to that place. But his experiences had caused him to drift away from Plato's teachings toward a more scientific approach to life. In other words, he now drew conclusions from what he discovered in the physical world around him.

So Aristotle went across town and created a new school called the Lyceum on the northeast side of Athens just outside the city walls. His long-term friend and assistant Theophrastos joined him there, which freed him from much of the teaching and administrative demands on his time. That allowed Aristotle to spend considerable amounts of effort writing the many innovative books and papers that proceeded to flow from his pen.

He also kept in touch by letter with his favorite student, Alexander, whose actions were already starting to bring a measure of glory to all of Greece.

THE ETERNAL LEGACY

The difficulties Alexander faced in the days after he received his crown were staggering. At only twenty years of age he sat on a throne stained by his father's blood. And some believed his mother was the force behind that murder. Intra-family intrigues caused several more relatives to perish, but the sword did not fall on Alexander.

In the midst of these deadly games he tried to pick up the reins of this large and scattered kingdom that his father had assembled by force. But those earlier battles left angry people in their wake, and each day brought new word of rebellions against his rule. From the semi-subjected cities of Athens and Thebes all the way to towns in Thessaly and Thrace, there were signs of revolt. If that was not enough, Alexander felt possessed by a desire to attack Persia, the largest and most powerful empire on earth. It was as if David was setting out to face not only Goliath but a circle of other enemies as well.

Yet Alexander never seemed to doubt himself. He drew upon the depths of Greek culture in which he had been raised, and its

Fig. 65 Alexander the Great

many philosophical and military traditions. Then he simply set out to do what needed to be done.

He went into the heartland of Greece with a cavalry unit of only 3,000 men and defeated the Thessalians. Then he accepted new declarations of loyalty from Athens, Corinth and other Greek cities. With those in place, he headed north and dealt with Thrace. Yet no sooner was he gone than Thebes and Athens rebelled once again. So Alexander returned and leveled Thebes to the ground. Athens got the message, and there was no further trouble.

Having set his house in order, Alexander gathered the best troops available to him and launched his campaign against Persia. He crossed the Hellespont into Asia in 334 BC with only 48,100 soldiers, 6,100 cavalry and 120 ships.[123] The enemy he faced could bring hundreds of thousands of troops to every battle. But he went anyway. Alexander quickly won victories at Granicus, Miletus, Halicarnassus and Termessos. He untied the Gordian knot with his sword, then went on to Issus at the northeast corner of the Mediterranean Sea where he defeated the Persian king Darius and his main army. A siege at Tyre delayed him, but then Alexander swept south into Egypt and founded the city of Alexandria on the coast as his new Greek capital for that country.

Going to Mesopotamia, he fought Darius once again, this time at Gaugamela in what is now northern Iraq. Once again Darius was defeated. With that, the war for Persia was essentially over, and Alexander marched victorious into Babylon, Susa and Persepolis. But to confirm his rule he chased remnants of the Persian army into what is now Afghanistan, Pakistan, Tajikistan, Uzbekistan and the northern tip of India. Then he returned at last to Babylon.

The tragic death of his closest friend Hephaestion, a companion since his days in Aristotle's classroom, devastated Alexander. And it was not long before he was in failing health himself, suffering from poison or disease. Finally in the middle of 323 BC, at thirty-two years of age, he passed away.

Alexander had conquered all of the Persian empire. In doing so he and the Greek people gained a measure of revenge for the shocking destruction of Athens 157 years earlier. And in a strange turn of events, Athens still lived, while the Persian empire perished.

Yet even in death Alexander had a stature no one person could match. It was only after much in-fighting that his Hellenic empire was divided into four parts under different Greek rulers. His childhood friend Ptolemy became king of all the African lands, ruling from Alexandria in Egypt. Seleucus, one of Alexander's senior generals, became king of all the Asian lands, and ruled from Babylon. Lysimachus, another schoolmate of Alexander, ruled the bridge lands between Europe and Asia—essentially Thrace and Anatolia—from the city of Pergamon. Another senior general, Antigonus, ruled Macedonia and exercised some measure of control over the Greek city-states, residing in the city of Pella in Macedonia.

For Aristotle, the passing of Alexander meant the end of letters from his most famous student. Those writings had sometimes been accompanied by unique animals and plants from those far-off places—anything that might bring some enjoyment and sense of wonder to Alexander's patient teacher.

When confirmation of the young man's death arrived, it no doubt caused Aristotle a sincere feeling of loss. And perhaps also a sense of amazement at how the Greek heritage he had imparted to Alexander had become spread so far across the world.

In terms of the people around him in Athens, it seemed they were flourishing anew. With the Persians completely removed from the Aegean Sea, and with all the Greek cities from Phocis to Miletus free to resume their Greek ties and trade, tremendous benefits accrued to Athens and all those other cities. This bounty encouraged students to continue flowing into his Lyceum, among other cultural pursuits.

Even so, it was only a year later that Aristotle taught his final lecture. With his dying breaths he called Theophrastos, his longtime friend and colleague, and conferred his legendary school and teachings into the man's care.

It seemed like the end of an era. The legacy of Aristotle now joined that of Socrates and Plato, Aeschylus and Euripides, Herodotus and Thucydides, Pericles and Aspasia, along with all the others who had contributed to the golden age of Athens.

Among the many strong attributes that made them memorable, there were a few that kept recurring. And none of those was more striking than the ability to overcome obstacles and difficulties placed in their way. That seemed to become one of the mainstays in Greek life during those days. The whole city of Athens went through that many times over the years, from Marathon to Salamis and from Pylos to Aegina. After each difficult challenge the city emerged stronger and in more beautiful array than the time before.

Even simple moments that did not garner great praise in the annals of history glowed in private triumph. Such a moment was seen in 459 BC when all the able-bodied soldiers of Athens were away at war and a threatening host of the enemy suddenly appeared in nearby Megara. Those who were too old to fight or too young to fight had set out from Athens and faced what had to be faced. Against all expectations, they carried the day. These old and young Athenians returned home not to the same glory they once had, but to a greater glory.

This was the heritage they passed on to their children—to take the burden of a heavy stone from their shoulder and place it at their feet. Then step up onto the stone and rise to greater heights than they had ever known before.

AFTERWORD

The change Athens experienced—from a city devastated by the Persians to a center of arts, culture and society in its golden age—was truly remarkable. The light that it lit was so bright that it can still be seen today, more than two thousand years later. Even the names of her leading citizens and aspects of their lives are known to us now, as are the obstacles they had to overcome to achieve their lasting accomplishments.

Without a doubt they did not give us a perfect world, and we still wrestle with our own difficulties today. But they did give us time-proven examples of how to overcome obstacles in front of us—and how to emerge better for having gone through that experience.

One of the most serious obstacles we face today is the economic hardship afflicting large numbers of people in societies around the world. This burden has fallen especially hard on the Greek people. The debt crisis that they faced beginning in 2010 prompted a wave of well-intended international bailout offers, but with those offers came strict austerity demands that heaped even greater loads onto the already-suffering Greek people. Unemployment soared. Large

Fig. 66 Austerity protests in Athens

public protests sprang up across the country. A downward spiral began in which people who had worked their whole life found they were suddenly without a job. And without work, there was no money to buy food or pay the rent.

When the people of ancient Athens returned home to find that the Persians had torn down all their buildings and burned what was left, they did not sit long among the ashes. Their leaders exhorted them forward and they immediately began to rebuild. They built new homes for shelter. They built a solid wall for protection. They built city forums to preserve their Greek way of life. And they did not stop there. Having learned once again how to come together and make their life better, they built architectural wonders such as the Parthenon and populated them with statues and artworks of surpassing beauty. They built monumental theatres and filled them with dramas about the life they lived. And they built creative works of philosophy and science that paved the way for all the generations that followed.

Their experiences provided clear guidelines about how to dig in and begin—then keep persevering until the whole community has built a better place in which to live. It did not happen overnight. And it was not easy, nor without setbacks along the way. But they got there.

There is much to learn from the people of Athens and their rise to the greatness of their golden age.

*Dedicated
to Athena*

*and to all who
love her.*

APPENDIX

ILLUSTRATION ACKNOWLEDGEMENTS

Images without captions

The Ancient Greek World in the Fifth Century BC — original drawing by Sanford Holst. **(Map)**

Frontispiece — The Greek poet Pindar — original photo by Stas Kozlovsky/CC-BY-SA-3.0.

Appendix — original photo was by Sanford Holst.

Figure

1. *Theseus slaying the Minotaur* – original bronze sculpture was by Antoine-Louis Barye (1843).
2. *Large krator from Euonymeia, circa 725 BC* – original photo was by Marie-Lan Nguyen/CC-BY-2.5.
3. *Solon* – original bust in the Musée national archéologique de Naples.
4. *Dionysos* – original photo was by Marie-Lan Nguyen/CC-BY-2.5.
5. *King Nestor and his sons, believed to be ancestors of Peisistratos, shown on an Attica krater* – original photo was by Marie-Lan Nguyen/CC-BY-2.5.
6. *Satyr on an Attica plate, circa 520-500 BC* – original photo was by Bibi Saint-Pol.

Figure

7. *Temple of Olympian Zeus* – original photo was by Greenshed.
8. *Pericles' Family–The Alcmaeonids* – original graphic by Sanford Holst.
9. *The Oracle at Delphi* – original kylix was by the Kodros painter (440-430 BC), appearance enhanced by Sanford Holst.
10. *Cleisthenes* – original photo was by www.ohiochannel.org.
11. *Greece at the outbreak of the Persian War* – original drawing by Sanford Holst. **(Map)**
12. *Greek helmet from the Battle of Marathon and the skull found inside it* — original photo was by Keith Schengili-Roberts/CC-BY-SA-2.5.
13. *Miltiades* — original drawing by Evald Hansen, published in *Illustrerad Verldshistoria* by Ernst Wallis in 1875.
14. *One of the ostraka votes cast against Xanthippus along with a collection of ostraka votes cast in various years* – (top) original photo was by Giovanni Dall' Orto, (bottom) original photo was by Sanford Holst.
15. *Themistocles* – original drawing by Evald Hansen, published in *Illustrerad Verldshistoria* by Ernst Wallis in 1875.
16. *King Leonidas and the Spartans before the final battle of Thermopylae* – original painting by Jacques-Louis David in 1814.
17. *Greek hoplite soldier fights a Persian in this picture from the bottom of a kylix drinking cup* – by the Triptolemos painter, circa 480 BC.
18. *Anaxagoras* – original fresco was by Eduard Lebiedzki (1888), after a design by Carl Rahl, enhanced by Sanford Holst.
19. *A prostitute is paid for sex on this wine vessel circa 430 BC* – original photo was by Marsyas/CC-BY-SA-2.5.
20. *North wall of the Acropolis with round columns from old temples built into the wall* – original photo was by Sanford Holst.
21. *Cimon* – original photo was by Markus Leupold-Lowenthal/CC-BY-SA-3.0.
22. *Campaigns in the Aegean and Anatolia* – original drawing by Sanford Holst. **(Map)**
23. *The speaker's platform on Pnyx Hill* – original photo, taken in 1865-1895, courtesy of Cornell University Library/CC-BY-2.0.
24. *Pericles* – original photo was by Jastrow.
25. *The Argolis campaigns* – original drawing by Sanford Holst. **(Map)**
26. *Athena Promachos as shown on an Athenian amphora* – original photo was by Ricardo André Frantz/CC-BY-SA-3.0.
27. *Aspasia* – marble bust in Vatican Museum, original photo was by Jastrow.

Figure

28. *Prize amphora for Panathenaic footrace circa 500 BC* – by the Kleophrades Painter, original photo was by Jastrow, enhanced by Sanford Holst.
29. *Cavalry in the Panathenaia procession, as shown on the marble frieze of the Parthenon* – original photo was by Jastrow.
30. At t*his archway in the city wall, the Eridanos River flowed out of Athens near the Dipylon Gate* – original photo was by Sanford Holst.
31. *The Agora of Classical Athens* – original drawing was by Madmedea/CC-BY-SA-2.0, enhanced by Sanford Holst.
32. *Map of Classical Athens city walls and districts* – original drawing in public domain, enhanced by Sanford Holst.
33. *The city walls completely surrounded Athens* – original image was by Gfmichaud/CC-BY-SA-3.0, enhanced by Sanford Holst.
34. *The Acropolis as seen from the air* – original photo was by Dale K. Bennington at HMdb.org, enhanced by Sanford Holst.
35. *Temple of Hephaistos* – original photo was by Sanford Holst.
36. *Herodotus* – original photo was by Marie-Lan Nguyen/CC-BY-3.0.
37. *The Parthenon* – original photo was by Steve Swayne/CC-BY-2.0.
38. *Pericles, Socrates and Aspasia discussing philosophy* – original painting was by Nicolas-André Monsiau (1754 - 1837).
39. *Aeschylus* – photographer unknown (1905).
40. *Sophocles* – original photo was by Shakko/CC-BY-SA-3.0.
41. *Euripides* – original photo was by Marie-Lan Nguyen.
42. *Aspasia* – original painting was by Marie-Genevieve Bouliard (1794).
43. *Aspasia admires the Acropolis* – original painting was titled *Aspasia on the Pnyx,* by Henry Holiday (1888).
44. Propylaia entrance to the Acropolis — drawing from *Pierers Konversations-Lexicon* (1891), enhanced by Sanford Holst.
45. *Brandenburg Gate in Berlin emulated the Propylaia* – original photo was by Fersy/CC-BY-2.0.
46. *A slave girl attending to her mistress in Athens* – original photo was by Matthias Kabel/CC-BY-SA-2.5.
47. *Socrates* – marble bust in the Louvre Museum, original photo was by Sting/CC-BY-SA-2.5.
48. *Phidias* – original painting was titled "The Apotheosis of Homer" by Jean-Auguste-Dominique Ingres (1827), enhanced by Sanford Holst.
49. *The Eleusinian Mysteries are portrayed on this tablet found in the sanctuary at Eleusis* – original photo was by Marsyas/CC-BY-2.5.

Figure

50. *Pericles delivering the funeral oration* – original painting was by Philipp Foltz (1877).
51. *Hippocrates* – original engraving was by Peter Paul Rubens (1638), courtesy of the National Library of Medicine.
52. *Athenians return from Salamis rejoicing* – original drawing was by Fernand Cormon (1845-1924).
53. *Thucydides* – original photo was by shakko/CC-BY-SA-3.0.
54. *Socrates Drags Alcibiades from the House of Aspasia* – original painting was by Jean-Baptiste Regnault (1791).
55. *Erechtheion Temple and the Caryatids* – original photo was by Thermos/CC-BY-SA-2.5.
56. *Alcibiades* – original photo was by Marie-Lan Nguyen.
57. *Cities of Sicily and Magna Graecia* – original drawing by Sanford Holst. **(Map)**
58. *Alcibiades and his courtesans* – original painting by Félix Auvray (1800-1833).
59. *Thrasybulus receiving an olive crown in Athens* – original drawing from Andrea Alciato's *Emblemata* (1531), enhanced by Sanford Holst.
60. *Xenophon* – original photo was by unknown person (1905).
61. *Plato* – original photo was by Tetraktys/CC-BY-SA-3.0.
62. *Socrates drinks the fatal hemlock* – original painting was titled "Death of Socrates" by Jacques-Louis David (1787).
63. *Aristotle* – marble bust in National Museum of Rome, original photo was by Jastrow.
64. *King Philip II of Macedon, father of Alexander the Great* – original photo was by Gunnar Bach Pederson.
65. *Alexander the Great* – original photo was by Tkbwikmed.
66. *Austerity protests in Athens* – original photo was by Ggia/CC-BY-SA-3.0.

ANNOTATIONS

1 Pindar, "Pythians Ode I" in *The Odes of Pindar in English Prose, Volume I*, translated by Gilbert West (Oxford: Munday, Slatter & Whittaker, 1824), p. 131.

2 Much of that original wall has been replaced by subsequent building projects, but a portion of it can still be seen on the northwest side of the Acropolis.

3 His name comes to us from the traditional king-list of the city. This list seems to combine reality with mythology, since Athena, Hephaestos and other gods and goddesses are given roles in the birth, life and death of these kings.

4 The classical theater stands just west of the Leof. Vouliagmenis highway, on Archeou Theatrou street. The hilltop "acropolis" is known as the Geroulanou Estate and is about 250 yards west of the theatre. The northern site is referred to as Kontopigado and is located immediately west of the Leof. Vouliagmenis highway at Dim. Gounari street.

[5] The year in which any particular event occurred in ancient Greece may be stated differently in different texts, so only the date most often cited is used here. This is most frequently due to events being recorded as taking place when a specific man was *archon eponymos* of Athens. Since the archonship traditionally started in July and ended the following June, it is not clear whether the event happened at the end of one year or the beginning of the next. Or an event might only be known to have happened before or after another event, giving a range of possible years. Although the dates shown throughout this work are as precise as allowed by the facts, some scholars may offer different opinions.

[6] Although Solon's reforms are often attributed to his year as *archon*, it is possible that they came twenty-two years later when he was a senior member of the Areopagus. That year would be 571 BC. I suggest this because the next year after making his reforms he met pharaoh Amasis II in Egypt, and that man did not become pharaoh until 570 BC.

[7] Draco's laws were implemented in 622/1 BC.

[8] Aristotle *Aristotle on the Athenian Constitution* translated by Fredrick G. Kenyon (London: G. Bell, 1904), pp. 1-126. However some modern historians are inclined to believe that the *boule* was created at another time.

[9] Herodotus *The Histories*, translated by Robin Waterfield (Oxford: Oxford University Press, 1998) 1:30.

[10] Plutarch *Plutarch's Lives*, translated by Dryden and A.H. Clough (Boston: Little, Brown & Co., 1895) Vol. I, p. 194.

[11] Their mothers were said to be cousins, but Peisistratos was much younger. *Plutarch's Lives: Solon 1:2.*

[12] Plutarch *Plutarch's Lives*, translated by John Dryden, edited by A.G. Clough (Boston: Little, Brown & Co., 1895) Vol. I, pp. 199-200.

[13] This god would later be adopted by the Romans, who changed his name to Dionysus. In the original Greek form, however, his name was Dionysos.

[14] Simon, Erika *Festivals of Attica* (Madison, WI: University of Wisconsin Press, 1983), p. 102.

[15] Carpenter, Thomas H. *Dionysian Imagery in Fifty-Century Athens* (Oxford: Clarendon Press, 1997), pp. 18, 93 and 108.

[16] Mahr, August C. *The Origin of the Greek Tragic Form* (New York: Prentice-Hall, 1938), p. 15.

[17] This Hippocrates was not the famous physician. Hippocrates was a common name in ancient Athens.

[18] Herodotus *The Histories* 5:65.

[19] Herodotus *The Histories*, translated by Robin Waterfield (Oxford: Oxford University Press, 1998), p. 26.

[20] Herodotus *The Histories* 1:61-64.

[21] Norwood, Gilbert *Greek Tragedy* (London: Methuen & Co., 1920/1953), p. 60.

[22] Mahr, August C. *The Origin of the Greek Tragic Form* (New York: Prentice-Hall, 1938), p. 16.

[23] Although this building is often called the Enneakrounos—the main fountainhouse built by Peisistratos—that honor may belong to a different building south of the Acropolis.

[24] Her name was Agariste, mother of the famous Cleisthenes.

[25] The rigorously-followed rule in naming children among Athens' leading families was that the first son was always named after the most prominent of the child's grandfathers. In this case that would be Hippocrates of the much-honored Alcmaeonid family. The second son was then named after the other grandfather, in this case Ariphron, the father of Xanthippus. The third son could then be given any name desired by the family. In this family, two sons survived childhood—Ariphron and Pericles, with Ariphron reportedly being the older of the two. This would have only been possible if the first-born son, who would have been named Hippocrates, died at an early age. That also would explain why Pericles was not named after either grandfather, but was given a name of his own.

[26] Different sources provide varying estimates of troop strength, but the Persians were believed to have had about 25,000 regular infantry and cavalry, with 100,000 armed sailors behind them.

[27] Miller, Stephen G. *Ancient Greek Athletics* (New Haven: Yale University, 2006), pp. 45-46.

28 This process was called *ostracism* because votes were cast by writing a name on a piece of broken pottery or *ostrakon*. Thousands of these pieces of pottery have been found in Athens with the names of *ostracized* men written on them.

29 Election in Classical Athens could be by lot or by hand, depending on the office and the laws in place at the time. Military offices tended to be elected by hand since their performance was critical. Archons tended to be elected by lot from among proposed candidates.

30 The rich vein of silver was discovered at Maronia, which is today called Agios Konstantinos, just inland from the mines of ancient Laurion.

31 Aristotle *Aristotle on the Athenian Constitution,* translated by Fredrick G. Kenyon (London: G. Bell, 1904) pp. 1-126.

32 Herodotus *The Histories* 7:32.

33 Herodotus *The Histories* 9:13.

34 Plutarch *Plutarch's Cimon and Pericles,* translated by Bernadotte Perrin (New York: Charles Scribner's Sons, 1910), Section VII, pp. 110-111.

35 This major hurdle of being enrolled on the *deme* list was accomplished at age eighteen. Then additional rights were awarded over time. After completing military training for two years, each 20-year-old citizen was allowed to attend the assembly and vote there, with other rights coming later. See Sinclair, R.K. *Democracy and Participation in Athens* (Cambridge: Cambridge University Press, 1988), p. 31.

36 The poet Sappho of Lesbos wrote extensively about love between women, but little of her work was preserved.

37 Plutarch *Plutarch's Lives, Vol. 5,* translated by Sir Thomas North (London: J.M. Dent, 1899), p. 143.

38 Kagan, Donald *Pericles of Athens and the Birth of Democracy* (New York: The Free Press, 1991), p. 38.

39 Boardman, John editor, *The Cambridge Ancient History Vol. V* (Cambridge: Cambridge University Press, 1992), p. 75

40 Kagan, Donald *Pericles of Athens and the Birth of Democracy* (New York: The Free Press, 1991), p. 49.

---

[41] A major source for these accounts of specific events during the First Peloponnesian War is Thucydides' *History of the Peloponnesian War*, particularly 1:102 onward.

[42] Herodotus *The Histories* 8:46.

[43] Kagan, Donald *Pericles of Athens and the Birth of Democracy* (New York: The Free Press, 1991), p. 177.

[44] Plutarch *Lives: Pericles* 13:9-12

[45] The other spelling used for his name is Pheidias, and both forms have come to be accepted.

[46] The date for *Athena Promachos* being installed on the Acropolis is usually given as 456 BC, though slightly later dates have also been suggested. The generally accepted view of this statue shows her spear held aloft beside her head and pointed forward, though she has also been portrayed holding the spear at her side with its point facing upward.

[47] Although they attracted less notice, Erythrea and Colophon are believed to have also stopped making payments at this time and were similarly chastised, as several other cities had been in the past.

[48] Nails, Debra *The People of Plato* (Indianapolis: Hackett Publishing, 2002), p.59. Nails and Peter K. Bicknell go on to confirm this relationship between Alcibiades and Aspasia by using the gravestones of descendants as evidence.

[49] The white-marble Panathenaic Stadium was rebuilt several times over the years, most notably in 1896 so the first modern Olympic Games could be held there.

[50] Some believe that a Roman temple located to the west stands on the site of the temple to Aphrodite. To see the altar—and the Painted Stoa beside it—look immediately north of modern Adrianou Street.

[51] Note that buildings erected after 450 BC are not included in this walk through the Agora. They are mentioned later, and described in the year they are built.

[52] To meet this around-the-clock requirement the 50 *prytaneis* members divided themselves into three groups of 16 or 17 people, with each group being on duty in the Tholos for eight hours a day.

[53] For further details on the structures under the Bouleuterion and Tholos, see Camp, John M. *The Athenian Agora* (London: Thames and Hudson, 1986), pp. 39-45.

[54] Miller, Stephen G. *The Prytaneion: Its Function and Architectural Form* (Berkeley: University of California Press, 1978). Also Schmalz, Geoffrey C. R. "The Athenian Prytaneion Discovered?" *Hesperia: The Journal of the American School of Classical Studies at Athens* Vol. 75, No. 1 (Jan. - Mar., 2006), pp. 33-81. Retrieved on July 12, 2016 from www.jstor.org/stable/25067975.

[55] Excavations that began in 2004 discovered a treasury of about 400 silver tetradrachm coins hidden in this building, suggesting that it may have served as the city Poleterion at some point. The *poletai* were responsible for state contracts, leases of silver mines, and taxes—all of which involved large amounts of money.

[56] Some also thought this location might have been used as a prison, even while noting there were other sites around the city that might have served as courthouses or prisons as well.

[57] For a full discussion of how the Aiakeion came into being, see Stroud, Ronald S. "The Athenian Grain-Tax Law of 374/3 BC" in *Hesperia* (Princeton: The American School of Classical Studies at Athens, 1998) Supplement 29.

[58] This building has frequently been identified as Enneakrounos, but experts have also pointed out several other sites that could fit the description for that building in ancient texts. Since Enneakrounos means "nine water-spouts" it is entirely possible that there were nine such fountainhouses in the city.

[59] The *demes* or districts of Athens within its thick walls were as follows. The number of representatives they sent to the city council are also shown, reflecting the size of their population. Melite (7), Kerameis (6), Skambonidai (3), Kydathenaion (12), Kollytos (3), Koile (3). See Traill, John S. *The Political Organization of Attica: A Study of the Demes, Trittyes, and Phylai, and their Representation in the Athenian Council* (Princeton: American School of Classical Studies at Athens, 1975).

[60] Müller, Karl *Attica and Athens,* translated by John Ingram Lockhart (London: Groombridge, 1842), p. 114.

[61] Dinsmoor, William Bell *The Architecture of Ancient Greece* (New York: Biblio and Tannen, 1928), pp. 90-91.

[62] In fact an olive tree still grows today in that same spot on the Acropolis.

[63] It is not clear whether there was a formal document signed at this time or if there was simply an understanding that there would be no further attacks between Greeks and Persians.

[64] Kagan, Donald *Pericles of Athens and the Birth of Democracy* (New York: The Free Press, 1991), p. 174.

[65] At a later date Herodotus' long and detailed history was divided into nine books to make the material more manageable.

[66] Billheimer, Albert *Naturalization in Athenian Law and Practice* (Gettysburg, PA: Princeton doctoral thesis, 1917), p. 12.

[67] Perry, Anna Louise, and Alfred Emerson, "The Dimensions of the Athena Parthenos" *The American Journal of Archaeology and of the History of the Fine Arts* Vol. 11, No. 3 (Jul. - Sep., 1896), pp. 335-349.

[68] Description is based on the Varvakeion Athena, a marble copy of the original statue made in the 2nd century CE, currently on display in the National Archaeological Museum of Athens.

[69] This happened in 457 BC. The other northern states were Locris and Phocis—whose cities included Delphi, home of the famous oracle.

[70] As shown here, Pericles led the armies of Athens on several expeditions over the years, which indicated that he was chosen to be one of the ten *strategos* or generals of the army who were elected in those years. Yet in 444/3 BC, when he was elected *strategos* again, he began what would be an extraordinary record of successful election to this important office every year for the rest of his life.

[71] The "Thirty Years Peace" ended what was known as the First Peloponnesian War, but it did not last for the promised thirty years. In 431 BC the Second Peloponnesian War began.

[72] Hippodamus of Miletus wrote his treatise *The Urban Planning Study for Piraeus* in 451 BC.

[73] Plato. "Menexenus" *Plato in Twelve Volumes, Vol. 9,* translated by W. R. M. Lamb (Cambridge, MA: Harvard University Press, 1925), Section 235e.

[74] Kagan, Donald *Pericles of Athens and the Birth of Democracy* (New York: The Free Press, 1991), p. 106-107.

[75] The City Dionysia was held around the time of the vernal equinox each year (toward the end of March), three months after the Rural Dionysia.

[76] There was even a separate festival called the Lenaia which began offering comedy competitions in 442 BC, then added tragedies later. It was held in January about the same time as—or shortly after—the Rural Dionysia.

[77] The surviving plays of **Aeschylus** are *The Persians* (472 BC), *Seven against Thebes* (467 BC), *The Suppliants* (463 BC), *Prometheus Bound* (which some experts feel may actually have been written by his son Euphorion), and three plays which together are known as the *Oresteia* in 458 BC: *Agamemnon, The Libation Bearers (Choephori),* and *Eumenides.*

[78] *Anthologiae Graecae Appendix, vol. 3, Epigramma sepulcrale.* p. 17.

[79] The surviving plays of **Sophocles** are *Ajax, Antigone* (442 BC), *Trachiniae, Oedipus the King (Oidipous Tyrannos,* after 429 BC), *Elektra, Philoctetes* (409 BC), and *Oedipus at Colonus* (produced in 401 BC by his grandson).

[80] The surviving plays of **Euripides** are *Alcestis* (438 BC), *Medea* (431 BC), *The Children of Heracles (Heraclidae), Hippolytus* (428 BC), *Andromache, Hecuba, Suppliants, Ion, Electra, Mad Heracles (Heracles Mainomanos), Trojan Women* (415 BC), *Iphigenia in Tauris, Helen* (412 BC), *Phoenician Women, Orestes* (408 BC), *Bacchae* (406 BC), *Iphigeneia at Aulis* (406 BC), *Rhesus,* and *Cyclops* (a satyr play).

[81] The surviving plays of **Aristophanes** are *Acharnians* (425 BC), *Knights* (424 BC), *Clouds* (423 BC), *Wasps* (422 BC), *Peace* (421 BC), *Birds* (414 BC), *Lysistrata* (411 BC), *Women of the Thesmophoria (Thesmophoriazusae,* 411 BC), *Frogs* (405 BC), *Women of the Assembly (Ecclesiazusae,* 393 BC), and *Plutus* (388 BC).

[82] Plutarch *Plutarch's Lives* translated by Sir Thomas North (London: J. M. Dent & Co., 1898) Vol. II, p. 160-163.

[83] Another reason cited for why Athens entered this conflict was the fact that Miletus had been defeated by Athens eleven years earlier and was left defenseless, so Athens felt obliged to provide their defense. It was also suggested that Athens was coming to the aid of a fellow democracy at Miletus which was being attacked by an outside oligarchy.

[84] The Goths and Herulae, in 267 AD.

[85] Some sources say it was his son Attalus II.

[86] Herodotus *The Histories* 6:137

[87] Finley, Moses et al. *Economy and Society in Ancient Greece* (London: Chatto and Windus, 1981).

[88] Plato, "Symposium, Book II, 219e-221b" *Great Dialogues of Plato,* translated by W.H.D. Rouse (New York: Mentor, 1984).

[89] Plutarch *Plutarch's Lives,* translated by John Dryden, edited by A.G. Clough (Boston: Little, Brown & Co., 1882), Vol. I, p. 416.

[90] The two philosophers were Parmenides and Zeno. Plato's entire dialogue *Parmenides* is about this encounter.

[91] Plutarch *Plutarch's Cimon and Pericles,* translated by Bernadotte Perrin (New York: Scribner's Sons, 1910). 32:3.

[92] It was once thought that Phidias had been committed to jail after his trial, but now scholarship leans toward the sentence of exile, similar to the *ostracism* that several other great Athenians had endured .

[93] In the ancient calendar of classical Athens, the month was identified as Anthesterion.

[94] In the Athens calendar, this month was identified as Boedromion.

[95] The daughter is sometimes called Kore, the maiden.

[96] Another conflict between Athens and Corinth had taken place the previous year, the Battle of Sybota near the island of Corfu. This was another contributing conflict leading up to the Peloponnesian War.

[97] Thucydides *History of the Peloponnesian War,* translated by Rex Warner (New York: Penguin Books, 1972), Book II sections 36-41, pp. 144-148. Thucydides made it clear that Pericles spoke like this, instead of saying he used these exact words. This suggests Thucyd-

ides heard the speech and then wrote it down to the best of his recollection, and possibly consulted the recollection of others as well.

[98] Queijo, Jon *Breakthrough* (New Jersey: FT Press, 2010), pp. 11-12.

[99] At one time it was thought that old city walls may have existed as far out as the Themistocles walls that came later, but the only walls that have been found are much closer to the Acropolis. See Papadopoulos, John K. "The Archaic Wall of Athens: Reality or Myth?" *Opuscula 1.* (Stockholm: Swedish Institutes at Athens and Rome, 2008), pp. 31-46.

[100] Plato, "Symposium (220d-221c)" *Great Dialogues of Plato,* translated by W.H.D. Rouse (New York: Mentor, 1984), pp. 114-115.

[101] Plutarch *Plutarch's Cimon and Pericles,* translated by Bernadotte Perrin (New York: Scribner's Sons, 1910), XXIV.

[102] Aspasia, Socrates and Alcibiades were seen together—or any two of them together—in paintings by Jean-Léon Gérôme, Jean-Baptiste Regnault, Christoffer Wilhelm Eckersberg, Michele Corneille the Younger, and others.

[103] The Caryatid statues that today stand watch from the porch of the Erechtheion are faithful copies of the originals. Five of those original Caryatids stand in the Acropolis Museum, while the sixth rests in the British Museum.

[104] Author's note—Given the events that transpired in Sicily, it is entirely possible that any of the three strategies proposed by the Athenian generals would have worked—if carried out by the person who created it. At first the leaders of Syracuse were unprepared and disorganized, so the sudden forceful attack proposed by Lamachus would almost certainly have succeeded. The timid approach of defeating tiny Selinus and going home, as Nicias advised, would at least have avoided any major disaster. The plan of Alcibiades, if it was fully carried out, would have brought additional local allies into a fight where events sometimes hung in the balance and a small added push could have moved the outcome toward Athens. But Alcibiades' plan was chosen, then he was removed from the battlefield—and the worst possible outcome took place.

[105] This satrap was Tissaphernes, who at that time governed all of Lydia and Caria.

[106] The Battle of Cyzicus in 410 BC.

[107] Diodorus Siculus, *Library* 13.52-53.

[108] Nails, Debra *The People of Plato* (Indianapolis: Hackett Publishing, 2002), p. 58-59.

[109] Aristotle *Athenian Constitution*, section 35.

[110] There may have been a second story on the South Stoa, given the large number of supporting columns and the interior wall which could easily have supported it.

[111] One of the rooms also had a narrow room beside it which may have served as a vestibule.

[112] A more picturesque account of Xenophon becoming a student of Socrates was given by Diogenes Laertius about 600 years later.

[113] Xenophon's Socratic dialogues were *Apology, Memorabilia, Symposium* and *Oeconomicus*. His historical works included *Anabasis, Cyropaedia, Hellenica, Agesilaus,* and the *Constitution of Sparta*.

[114] The year of Plato's birth is given by many sources as ranging from 430 BC to 424 BC. Since one of the most frequently mentioned dates is 427 BC and that falls in the middle of this range, it is the date used here.

[115] Timocracy—a government in which only property owners are allowed to participate in the decision-making.

[116] Oligarchy—government controlled by a small number of people distinguished by family ties, wealth, education, religious position, military position or other criterion.

[117] Tyranny—governed by an absolute ruler.

[118] The "early" dialogues of Plato have been identified as *The Apology, Crito, Charmides, Lesser Hippias, Greater Hippias, Laches, Lysis, Euthyphro, Ion, Gorgias,* and *Protagoras*.

[119] This was known as the Corinthian War and lasted from 395 to 387 BC.

[120] The "middle" dialogues of Plato have been identified as *Meno, Euthydemus, Cratylus, Phaedo, Phaedrus, Symposium, The Republic,* and *Parmenides*.

[121] The "later" dialogues of Plato have been identified as *Theaetetus, Sophist, Statesman, Philebus, Timaeus, Critias,* and *Laws*.

[122] This alliance was known as the League of Corinth, signed in 337 BC by virtually all the major Greek cities except Sparta, with Philip at its head.

[123] Roisman, Joseph and Ian Worthington *A Companion to Ancient Macedonia* (Malden, MA: Blackwell, 2010), p.192.

BIBLIOGRAPHY

Aristotle *Aristotle on the Athenian Constitution* (translated by Fredrick G. Kenyon) London: G. Bell, 1904.

Aristotle, "Poetics" *Aristotle in 23 Volumes, Vol. 23* (translated by W.H. Fyfe). Cambridge, MA: Harvard University Press, 1932.

Benton, William (publisher) *Aeschylus, Sophocles, Euripides, Aristophanes* Chicago: Encyclopedia Britannica, 1952.

Billheimer, Albert *Naturalization in Athenian Law and Practice* Gettysburg, PA: Princeton doctoral thesis, 1917.

Boardman, John editor, *The Cambridge Ancient History* Cambridge: Cambridge University Press, 1992.

Buck, Robert J. *Thrasybulus and the Athenian Democracy*. Stuttgart: Franz Steiner Verlag, 1998.

Camp, John M. *The Athenian Agora: Excavations in the Heart of Classical Athens* London: Thames and Hudson, 1986.

Carpenter, Thomas H. *Dionysian Imagery in Fifty-Century Athens* Oxford: Clarendon Press, 1997.

Cornford, F.M. *Greek Religious Thought: From Homer to the Age of Alexander* New York: AMS Press, 1969.

Davidson, James *Courtesans and Fishcakes*. New York: St. Martin's Press, 1997.

Dinsmoor, William Bell *The Architecture of Ancient Greece* New York: Biblio and Tannen, 1928.

Diodorus Siculus *Bibliotheca Historica, Vol. 11* (translated by C.H. Oldfather, et al.) London : Heinemann, 1933.

Fine, John V.A. *The Ancient Greeks—A Critical History*. Cambridge, Mass: Harvard University Press, 1983.

Finley, Moses et al. *Economy and Society in Ancient Greece*. London: Chatto and Windus, 1981.

Flaceliere, Robert *Daily Life in Greece at the Time of Pericles* (translated from French by Peter Green) London: Phoenix, 2002.

Flexner, Stuart Berg et al (ed.) *The Random House Dictionary of the English Language, Second Edition Unabridged.* New York: Random House, 1987.

Gagarin, Michael *The Oxford Encyclopedia of Ancient Greece and Rome* Oxford: Oxford University Press, 2010.

Grafton, Anthony (editor) *The Classical Tradition* Cambridge, MA: Harvard University Press, 2010.

Green, Peter *The Greco-Persian Wars* Berkeley: University of California Press, 1996.

Guthrie, W.K.C. *The Greeks and Their Gods* London: Methuen & Co., 1950.

Haigh, A.E. *The Tragic Drama of the Greeks* Oxford: Clarendon Press, 1896.

Hall, Jonathan M. *Ethnic Identity in Greek Antiquity* Cambridge: Cambridge University Press, 1997.

Henry, Madeleine M. *Prisoner of History: Aspasia of Miletus and Her Biographical Tradition.* New York: Oxford University Press, 1995.

Herodotus *The Histories* (translated by Robin Waterfield) Oxford: Oxford University Press, 1998.

Holst, Sanford *Phoenician Secrets: Exploring the Ancient Mediterranean.* Los Angeles: Santorini Publishing, 2011.

Kagan, Donald *Pericles of Athens and the Birth of Democracy* New York: The Free Press, 1991.

Lacey, Jim *First Clash: The Miraculous Greek Victory at Marathon and Its Impact on Western Civilization* New York: Bantam Books, 2011.

Lefkowitz, Mary R. and Maureen B. Fant *Women's Life in Greece and Rome: A Source Book in Translation.* Baltimore: John Hopkins University Press, 1992.

Mahr, August C. *The Origin of the Greek Tragic Form* New York: Prentice-Hall, 1938.

Miller, Stephen G. *Ancient Greek Athletics* New Haven: Yale University, 2006.

Müller, Karl *Attica and Athens* (Translated by John Ingram Lockhart) London: Groombridge, 1842.

Nails, Debra *The People of Plato* Indianapolis: Hackett Publishing, 2002.

Neils, Jenifer *Worshiping Athena: Panathenaia and Parthenon* Madison WI: University of Wisconsin Press, 1996.

Nepos, Cornelius *Lysander, Alcibiades, Thrasybulus, et al.* (Latin, with English notes by E.S. Shuckburgh) Cambridge: Cambridge University Press, 1896.

Norwood, Gilbert *Greek Tragedy* London: Methuen & Co., 1920/1953.

Otto, Walter F. *Dionysus: Myth and Cult* (translated by Robert B. Palmer) Bloomington, IN: Indiana University Press, 1965/1973.

Parke, H.W. *Festivals of the Athenians* London: Thames and Hudson, 1977.

Perry, Anna Louise, and Alfred Emerson "The Dimensions of the Athena Parthenos" *The American Journal of Archaeology and of the History of the Fine Arts* Vol. 11, No. 3 (Jul. - Sep., 1896).

Pindar *The Odes of Pindar in English Prose, Volume I* (translation by Gilbert West) Oxford: Munday, Slatter & Whittaker, 1824.

Plato "Menexenus" *Plato in Twelve Volumes, Vol. 9* (translated by by W.R.M. Lamb) Cambridge, MA: Harvard University Press, 1925.

Plato "Symposium" *Great Dialogues of Plato* (translated by W.H.D. Rouse) New York: Mentor, 1984.

Plutarch *Plutarch's Cimon and Pericles.* (translated by Bernadotte Perrin) New York: Scribner's Sons, 1910.

Plutarch *Plutarch's Lives* (translated by Dryden, A.H. Clough) Boston: Little, Brown & Co., 1895.

Plutarch *Plutarch's Nicias and Alcibiades.* (translated by Bernadotte Perrin) New York: Scribner's Sons, 1912.

Plutarch *Plutarch's Themistocles and Aristides.* (translated by Bernadotte Perrin) New York: Scribner's Sons, 1901.

Pomeroy, Sarah B. *Goddesses, Whores, Wives, and Slaves.* New York: Schocken Books, 1975/1995.

Queijo, Jon *Breakthrough* New Jersey: FT Press, 2010.

Raubitschek, A.E. and Gorham P. Stevens *The Pedestal of the Athena Promachos.* Retrieved on October 2, 2015 from the site www.ascsa.edu.gr/pdf/uploads/hesperia/146884.pdf.

Rehm, Rush *Greek Tragic Theatre* London: Routeledge, 1992.

Roisman, Joseph and Ian Worthington *A Companion to Ancient Macedonia* Malden, MA: Blackwell, 2010.

Simon, Erika *Festivals of Attica* Madison, WI: University of Wisconsin Press, 1983.

Thucydides *History of the Peloponnesian War* (translated by Richard Crawley) London: Longmans, Green and Co., 1874.

INDEX

Made in the USA
Middletown, DE
14 April 2023

28860306R00163